EVERYTHING
ALL AT ONCE

EVERYTHING ALL AT ONCE

A Memoir

Steph Catudal

HARPERONE

An Imprint of HarperCollinsPublishers

HarperCollins books may be purchased for educational, business, or sales promotional use. For information, please email the Special Markets Department at SPsales@harpercollins.com.

FIRST EDITION

Designed by Terry McGrath

Library of Congress Cataloging-in-Publication Data has been applied for.

ISBN 978-0-06-325313-1

24 25 26 27 28 LBC 7 6 5 4 3

For Dad, because it was you all along
And for Mum, because you gave me the space to find him

EVERYTHING
ALL AT ONCE

PROLOGUE

It's 3:00 a.m.

I am bundled in a fleece blanket in the front passenger seat of our silver Dodge Caravan. Dad is speeding eastbound down Highway 20, the throughway that runs across Montreal, still wiping sleep from his eyes as he rushes me to the hospital. I pull for air in ragged breaths but Dad stays calm, offering me sips from a carton of Nestle's strawberry milk with one hand, the other locked on the steering wheel while Glenn Frey croons on an old mix tape. I feel the sharpness of Canadian winter air drawing in from the window that Dad has rolled down with three broad strokes of his arm, hoping the cold would ease my asthma. The bitter wind turns the tip of my nose numb and I say so in a whisper. Dad puts the strawberry milk in his cup holder and places a warm hand on my cheek. I sink into his palm, the width of it cradling the entirety of my seven-year-old face. He looks at me and smiles with only a hint of fear behind his soft brown eyes as I cough, and cough, and cough.

"Take it easy," he sings. The city rushes by us but his eyes locked on mine.

"Take it easy."

Six years later I'm sitting in the same van but it's my dad bundled in bedding on his way to the hospital. Mum is speeding down the highway, both her hands gripping the wheel while my little brother and I stare at each other in silence. There is no calm offering extended across worn bucket seats, no gentle reminder to take it easy.

I am thirteen years old and my father is dying of lung cancer.

I watch our city rush by us as he coughs, and coughs, and coughs.

* * *

And I can still hear him cough. You never forget a sound like that—the kind that tears at your throat, the kind that sputters and drowns and leaves you gasping for breath on dry land.

I remember.

CHAPTER 1

I am awake.

The sound splits the night, a rolling thunder tearing through the hilted gray of twilight.

It's midnight in early June and a monsoon is brewing up from the Gulf of Mexico, making its way to our home in northern Arizona. I can hear a violent wind whipping through our backyard, twisting through the chalky limestone and looming pines that corral our lot on the forested outskirts of town. It rattles the windows and flips trash cans in the street as I wrestle with the sheets.

But above the storm, all I hear is that cough.

That fucking cough.

It hovers in the space between sleeping and waking. I sit up in bed, my hands searching for the sound like a child pulled from a dream, looking for something that was just right here.

Weren't you just right here?

It takes a moment to realize that I am not caught in an outdated nightmare, that it's my husband—not my father—coughing above the storm. The melody of my adolescence, remastered.

It is three months into the coronavirus pandemic when his cough first appears. It creeps up the stairs and into our bedroom, from the basement where he has been quarantined for the past seven days.

I hear it and remember everything in metastatic memory—the bed pans, the tray table littered with pill bottles, my father's sunken face and a distant gaze in eyes that were once so keen, so knowing.

It calls to me, sour and distinct.

I lay back on my pillow and focus on the gusts that shift my bedroom walls like creaking bones, whispering a truth I will come to know well: *There is growth in this pain.*

I try to ignore the gale force of my husband's emerging illness and its sinewy escalation.

It pulls. It stretches.

I used to love stormy nights, how the humbling elements demanded appreciation for our small home. The wind would howl and I'd sink under the blankets, deep in the comfort of bed while the rain came down in heavy sheets. It was nights like this that I would admit my gratitude for the gas stove that kept us warm despite occupying a third of our living room, or for the roof my husband Rivs had reshingled a few summers earlier, though I'd complained about wanting to spend our savings on a road trip to Mexico instead. I'd even sulked as he climbed a rusted ladder onto our roof, bringing up our oldest daughter, who was five at the time, while I sat on a chair in the dirt below them. But my petulant scowl turned into a smile as I watched Harper hand her dad the nails she held carefully between her lips, pursed the way he had taught her—the way my father had once taught me.

Built in the high-altitude mountain town of Flagstaff, our home was a thousand-square-foot post-and-beam backed by a half-acre lot of sloping clay, overgrown with centuries-old pine trees and wild rose bushes that hooked into our ankles with unforgiving barbs. We spent our first summer as homeowners weeding a thicket of thorny brush while Harper chased lizards through volcanic dirt and our newborn Iris slept in a Moses basket under the canopy of ponderosas. When the bushes returned with a vengeance the following spring, we adopted three Nubian dwarf goats from a nearby farm and never wrestled with wild roses again.

At the time we bought our house, Rivs was making a small income as an endurance athlete while attending grad school to become a physical therapist. To supplement the financial demands of a growing family, we took turns serving tables at night, alternating roles between student and parent during the day. Between late-night restaurant shifts, diaper changes, and academic essays, we somehow found the time for Rivs to train and for me to write—investments that were long shots in terms of cultivating sustainable careers, which neither of us had any intention of giving up. By the time our third daughter Poppy was born, the scheduling contortionism had paid off: I was taking small jobs as a freelance writer, and Rivs had made a successful career around endurance athletics.

One afternoon shortly after Poppy's birth, I came home to see Rivs sitting on our front porch, looking at his phone in confusion. Sweat was crusted onto his black running cap and mahogany mud was caked on his calves from hours spent in the high desert forest. As I climbed the steps towards him, he asked if I had ever heard of a company called *H and M*, forming the letters meticulously as though he'd never put them together before.

"Um, yes . . . ?" I said, thinking he was joking before quickly realizing he was not. "It's one of the biggest retail clothing chains in the world, Rivs."

"Oh," he shrugged. "I thought it was a Scandinavian furniture company, like IKEA or something. Anyways, I think they want me to be the face of their new sportswear line."

I laughed and shook my head, but it shouldn't have surprised me that he had never heard of H&M. Other than a few pairs of running shorts, Rivs's wardrobe was a variation of the same outfit he'd worn for almost two decades: brown leather boots, an earth-toned T-shirt, and a pair of faded Levi's he grew up wearing around New Mexico and eastern Oregon. Maybe if it was cold he'd slip on his Pendleton flannel, the same one he'd owned since high school, long before flannels were fashionable. But fashion was never something that interested him and shopping for clothes was out of the question. Perhaps the real question was why he thought a furniture company would want to sponsor an elite athlete in the first place.

A burly 170 pounds and standing six feet one inches tall, Rivs worked tirelessly to make running into a lucrative career though his natural build would have better suited him as a linebacker. It was striking, if not comical, to see him queue up at marathon starting lines—the way he towered over his slender competition with a big auburn beard, chiseled stomach, and the broad shoulders he tried to whittle down obsessively yet unsuccessfully.

Throughout his running career, his muscular frame was its own battleground. Though he had won a handful of marathons over the past several years, all anyone seemed to want to celebrate was his titian facial hair, legs, and abs. Even after placing sixteenth at the Boston Marathon in an impressive time of two hours and eighteen minutes—a qualifying standard for the Olympic trials—the praise he received was mainly centered around his physique.

The more hype his online persona generated, the more uncomfortable he felt in the spotlight. What he *wanted* was to become a great runner, but his growing notability was based more around his aesthetic than his performance as an athlete. Still, he understood that social media was a valuable tool in building a modern running career. For him it was a clear choice: work 9 to 5 in a clinic as a physical therapist or pursue the life of an endurance athlete.

Without much debate, he chose running, and he approached the sport the same way he approached each day—with unrelenting self-determination and a puritanical work ethic that verged on compulsive, his success as a runner derived more from resolve than talent.

He was disciplined and honest with his nutrition. He was dedicated and consistent with his training. In the spring and summer he'd wake at 3:00 a.m. to climb the twelve-thousand-foot saddle of Humphreys

Peak, racing to beat the lightning storms that normally rolled in by early afternoon and, more importantly, to catch the sunrise summit over a distant painted desert. In the fall and winter he'd run-commute to school, covering eleven miles in each direction down snow-covered roads, stocked with a few burritos and a backpack loaded with school supplies.

But if consistent, gentle work was his training philosophy, then his racing style was cutthroat. He raced aggressively, pushing his body far past normal human limits over the course of twenty-six miles and beyond. Soothed by the calm of nature and redemptive miles on foot, it wasn't unusual for him to be running for over five hours a day. "Small and steady deposits," he'd say.

When I was eight months pregnant with Harper, we moved to Costa Rica for my master's degree—both of us equally surprised by my pregnancy and acceptance to the small United Nations university.

Soon after our arrival to Ciudad Colón, a rural suburb of the capital San José, Rivs went for a run in the jungle that backed our rental house. When he hadn't come home nine hours later, I waddled out to find him, equipped with a headlamp, a sandwich, and a dry branch I picked up halfway down the driveway—just in case.

I marched towards the dense tree line, ignoring Rivs's advice not to worry unless he'd been gone for more than twelve hours. As the sun hovered low on the horizon, my mind ran wild with imagined tales of him lost and dehydrated, leaving me alone and near labor in a foreign country.

I was only a mile up the dirt road when he trotted out from a grove of mango trees, sweaty and smiling. He took one look at my headlamp and twig and burst into laughter.

"I thought you were lost!" I was relieved but defensive, trying to hide the sandwich sweating in a Ziplock between my taut stomach and the waistband of my maternity shorts.

"Nah, just a little dehydrated and a bit turned around. I could see home the whole time—I just couldn't figure out how to get there." He gathered my belly in his arms. "But I told you not to worry, babe. I always make it back."

"I know," I said, leaning into his broad chest.

Because it was true. He always made it back.

* * *

A week before his cough started, Rivs had come home from a Grand Canyon run weakened far beyond the general fatigue that often followed long miles on his feet.

Living in Flagstaff, the canyon's South Rim was just over an hour from our house—a route edged by rolling high desert forest and towering cinder cones that fell into gaping striations of eons-old rock. No matter how often we made that drive, we were continually humbled by both the magnificence of nature and the triviality of human existence. The gradient sandstone was a monolith of ancestral wisdom marking our fleeting-but-singular place in history, a fossilized relic of impermanence.

I had run down the Grand Canyon trails a handful of times, covering the eighteen-mile round trip to the Colorado River and back, coaxed along by patient friends and the promise of a cold beer at the end. Rivs, on the other hand, would immerse himself in the canyon as often as possible—sometimes multiple times a week. The copper switchbacks were his place of reverence and communion, and he almost always chose to run them alone. The layered rock was a church whose sacrament of sweat and solitude held the promise of his absolution somewhere at the bottom. And Lord how he searched and searched.

But tonight he just coughs and coughs.

I sink back into my pillow lulled by a hacking nostalgia, the thunder less a call to appreciation and more a pneumonic reminder of how quickly things fall apart. In its discord I hear my father's voice telling me he is mortal, long before I believe in mortality. The memory cries louder than any monsoon wind—a haunted tune of broken faith and metered time, of rattled windows and ruptured stillness on an otherwise peaceful street.

(Take it easy. Take it easy.)

CHAPTER 2

We were sitting around the kitchen table the evening my parents told us. Hot words billowed from their mouths like fumes from an exhaust pipe, alkaline and toxic, but no one could keep them from seeping out.

I was seated across from my older brother Dave, and next to me sat my little brother Phil. Dad was at the head of the table, flanked by Mum on one side and Rachel, the oldest of us four siblings, on the other. We were a reasonably functional middle-class family living in the suburbs of Montreal, and despite Rachel's propensity to sneak boys into her bedroom and Dave's knack for getting arrested for petty theft, we made it a point to eat dinner together every evening.

There was nothing unusual about that night. We were all in our six o'clock dinner spots with a pan of roast chicken in the middle of the table, a side of baked beans placed beside it in my late grandmama's Le Creuset. In every way it might have looked like just another Sunday meal. Maybe Dave, sixteen at the time, would be drunk and making faces at me from across the table. Maybe Mum would give Dad a knowing look the rest of us wouldn't quite catch, and Dad would shake his head and say "Oh, Dave" with loving concern. Maybe Rachel would be asking to take the car downtown with her friends this weekend and Dad would remind her that she had been grounded from the car after he'd caught Justin Manning hiding in her bedroom closet.

"You might be eighteen, but I can still ground you as long as you're living in this house, sweetie," he'd say. Maybe Phil, then ten years old, would be looking at me, giggling and not really knowing what we were all laughing about but joining in anyways.

But if you had been there that night, you would have felt the weight of it—words that hung in the air, far more oppressive than suburban teenage rebellion. You would have seen how my father's strong face had turned inward, folding in on itself like a set of cards ready to show its hand. You would have seen Dave's sober countenance, how Phil's mouth was set tight lipped, how Rachel asked for nothing.

You would have seen me sitting calmly. Hopeful and deep breathed, I was comforted by Mum's faith in miracles and Dad's promise to fight like hell.

I didn't even see the smoke.

Hope. Faith. Miracles. I believed every word. Back then, life was as simple as the songs I sang at Mormon church each Sunday: choose the right, have faith, and watch the miracles unfold.

I wasn't scared when, my god, I should have been. This was one of my biggest regrets, more than the scarcity of hugs and I love yous and goodbyes—that I was full of hope when I should have been steeling myself for death. That I lived on one end of the pendulum, oblivious to everything in between.

But I was only thirteen, a child still berthed in the divinity of my parents, still believing that life was fair and balanced.

I hadn't yet learned of the space between childhood faith and adolescent knowing, when we are still anchored to parents who try to stem the tide of growing up. Desperate to keep us safe they dam us in black and white, to stave off the treacherous river of gray.

But when a child reckons innocence with reality, the flood is sometimes irreparable. The levee breaks and we are swept downstream. We grope for dry land, trying to make sense of a world that does not carry us as swiftly as we were once taught. We tear at the banks between innocence and truth, desperate for the bridge only to find that there are no square angles. No straight lines across.

It all just bends.

A few years earlier, Dave rigged a pulley system for the treehouse Dad had built when we were little. The dying poplar leaves rustled their autumnal chorus as I helped my big brother load rocks inside two old paint buckets. I watched carefully as he tied them to a frayed rope using one of his fishing knots, stringing it over and through a tree branch that looked sturdy enough. One afternoon I emptied the rocks from one of the buckets to make way for my cassette player, forgetting to reload the weight before Phil decided to ride the pulley down. Phil took a running jump, intent on impressing us older siblings, only to have the bucket plummet to the ground so swiftly that Dave and I didn't know whether to cheer or call an ambulance. After a muted shriek, Phil jumped up and walked it off, hurt and disoriented but pretending he was okay. Dave and I cheered from the treehouse above, commenting on how our little brother was finally growing up.

Faith would soon begin to feel like that to me.

But there was no way I could have known this, so I stared calmly at the outdated maroon and turquoise wallpaper Dad had pasted to the kitchen wall last year while the word *cancer* floated through the air.

I was familiar with that noxious word. Seven years earlier, when he was three and I was six, Phil was diagnosed with acute lymphoblastic leukemia. In my home, cancer was uttered with reverence and disdain—hated but not to be angered.

Cancer was a few years of disturbed routine and long days in the Montreal Children's Hospital. It was Rachel sobbing headily over the kitchen table while my grandmama soaked her feet in a bowl of warm water, trying to calm her shaking body. It was Mum pulling clumps of toddler hair out from the bath drain with a smile on her face. It was Dad pleading to a god he didn't believe in, desperate to barter his own life for his son's. "*Please god, if you're real, take me instead.*" It was a bald brother who sat in bed playing video games with swollen fingers while I was cooped up in a classroom having to learn my times tables.

By the age of seven, Phil was in full remission of disease. The reintroduction of cancer into my life three years later was tainted by naivete and optimism, dammed or maybe damned by the reservoir of my mother's unfaltering faith.

Through the haze of hope I might have seen that at the age of forty-five, Dad had been diagnosed with stage IV adenocarcinoma—a nonsmoking-related lung cancer that had already metastasized throughout his body. I might have heard that the excessive tumor burden in his lungs and brain made any chance of survival a medical impossibility. I might have felt the desperation in my father's words that night, each one mouthed with the intention that accompanies reckoning with an early death.

But all these truths were obscured by faith. All of them, including this: the doctors had given him three months to live.

Three months of life for the kind of father you'd be proud to go to the public pool with, not only because you could point and say "that's my dad" when he did handstand flips off the high diving board, or because when the swim team coach called on him to fill in for the sixteen-and-older relay team he'd emerge from the men's locker room wearing a tight Speedo, walking in exaggerated strides through the poolside crowd like a boxer making his way to the ring. Mostly we were proud because after the swim meet he'd wrap us in warm towels and let us snuggle down in his lap, offering us snacks and maybe even an ice-cold Orange Crush from the concessions stand.

"That's my dad," I'd think, burrowing into his warm chest, a can of soda clutched in my small hands like treasure. "That's *my* dad."

And now here we were sitting around the kitchen table, my father's mouth holding twelve weeks like his own secret treasure.

But god would heal him. I just *knew* it. Heavenly Father heals the sick if you ask just right.

The only time I looked into my dad's eyes that night was by command, when he promised he'd be around for each of our birthdays over the next year.

Rachel.

Dave.

Phil.

Steph.

Steph.

Steph.

Back then I didn't think much of him saying my name. Now I wish I would have listened to the way it rolled off his tongue, how he'd said it as though a single word could carry a lifetime of love. I would have noticed how it begged to be savored, how it taught that even the shortest syllable can cradle a whole life, infinitely.

If I had known, I would have held on to it, let it linger.

I was too young to understand the nuance of impermanence, too young to recognize the subtle changes my father's sickness would make in our lives; how they would shift slowly but grow over time to become a part of us, like when Mum had quietly traded her kitten heels for a pair of old slippers.

She used to wear her heels on Friday nights when Dad would take the 6:00 p.m. train home from work. He'd hop onto the platform in his fitted suit and greet her with a bouquet of flowers. He'd present them to her with one hand and squeeze her backside with the other, whispering something coy in her ear. She'd pull back a bit and blush like a schoolgirl, glancing over to all us kids as we watched and giggled from the minivan in the train station parking lot. Then we'd drive home, Mom clutching Dad's hand from across the armrest as we fought in hushed tones.

Now she was clutching a basket full of pill bottles, cleaning bedsores, and learning how to use a medical lift to get Dad from bed to his wheelchair. She was spoon-feeding him with an unwavering hand and sponging his shrinking frame with a devotion verging on desperation, each stroke of her arm a hopeful prayer.

Stay here. Stay.

* * *

It is mid-July, a few months before he dies, that Dad has us congregate in the living room.

He wants us to watch him do a set of handstand push-ups. He is trying to reconcile the letting-go of his once-colossal body, trying to intimidate death by a show of brute force.

"See?" he says. His thinning biceps quiver as he steadies his breath with searching eyes. "Your dad's not as sick as they say he is."

And we all nod, believing him.

But he slipped into a coma in late October, on the afternoon of my fourteenth birthday, after handing me a card with DAD XOXO written in trembling script. I went to school that morning, the birthday card hidden in my bedroom closet while the autumn leaves crunched under my feet on my way to the bus stop. Because the seasons pay no mind to how desperately you're hanging on. Life cycles on, even when you're dying.

When I came home from school that day he wasn't alive anymore, but he wasn't dead, either. He was somewhere in between.

* * *

I was at Walmart with a friend when he died two days later. I'd like to say that I felt his departing spirit—that I had been filled with in-candescent peace while standing in the checkout aisle deciding which chocolate bar to buy. That in an instant, before making its way to the hereafter, his soul glowed brighter than the flicker of fluorescent lights overhead. That I had dropped the Kit Kat bar and shifted my eyes towards the ceiling, knowing that he was free from pain and flying off towards that "better place" everyone kept talking about.

These were the stories I would hear from the pulpit at church on Sundays, of hidden blessings and silver linings, of god's purpose and eternal families, spoken at first in reverent tones, then with increased fervor as my dad grew closer to death.

Being raised Mormon, I was taught to believe in miraculous healings and divine intervention, in the sanctity of life and the eternal joy that awaited us all after death.

But there was no heavenly comfort for me in Walmart, and I felt mostly apathy when Mum cornered me in the entryway of our home to tell me Dad was finally gone. No pained cry, no tears. Just a nod of my head as I glanced up at Mum, her eyes bloodshot but not teary, as though the tragic months had dried the well.

I didn't want her to feel my indifference. The love of her life was dead, withered before her eyes, soon to be packaged in a black body bag and carted to the morgue. And the coroners would leave a rose on his empty bed as a kind gesture or some cruel mockery of the things she would never hold again.

I ran a hand down her arm in consolation before walking towards Dad's makeshift hospice room, where we had once kept the computer. She opened her mouth to say something but instead gave me a hug and turned towards the kitchen to call the coroner.

There was no more pretending that I could be dammed from the harsh realities of life. I was no longer a callow child but not quite ready to understand the world, either. Unmoored from the comfort of black and white, I was now awash in a torrent of gray.

Faith did not move mountains. God did not heal the sick. Prayers were not answered. Parents were mortal, and even worse, fallible.

I walked into Dad's room half-expecting to see him propped up with pillows holding the *Montreal Gazette*. Every day for the past year I had waited quietly by his bed, watching the newspaper pages tremble while he strained his tired eyes to read the print. He'd lower the paper when he saw me from the corner of his eye, smiling weakly with teeth that now looked too big for his face.

But today he was lying flat on the hospital bed, his eyes half shut and his mouth twisted open as though he had tried hard to draw one last breath from this world.

My eyes followed the fleece throw that blanketed his body, accentuating all the pieces of him that had withered away. His face was sunken, with gray skin and protruding cheekbones, sharp as the heels Mum used to wear.

I reached down to touch his hand, now more out of curiosity than tenderness, but withdrew my finger quickly. His skin was cold and puckered at the seams like a cheap doll. It felt foreign—so unlike the hand that used to scratch my back at bedtime or guide my finger to point out constellations in the sky.

The bedside tray beside him showed no sign that he was gone, still strewn with pill bottles, bedsore dressings, and a bowl of untouched applesauce with a spoon balanced over it. Beyond the tray were the sliding glass doors that led to our backyard, and through them I could see the last hint of sunlight gleaming through the naked poplars where the treehouse stood, built when we were still children, tucked high between the branches.

CHAPTER 3

It was late afternoon, one week before his cough started, when Rivs left for the Grand Canyon. The cicadas had just begun their end-of-day chorus as Derrick Lytle pulled up to our house in a tan minivan, his bare foot, tinged copper from red rock sand, hanging out the driver's window.

Though Rivs usually ran the Grand Canyon alone, today he was joined by his adventure-videographer friend, who had come down from southern Utah to run a longer variation of the infamous Rim-to-Rim-to-Rim route. Their plan was to run across the canyon and back along Bright Angel Trail, a grueling forty-eight-mile trek of unforgiving terrain with over eleven thousand feet of climbing. A multiday bucket list journey for most hikers, this was a somewhat routine ten-hour run for Rivs and his endurance athlete friends.

Derrick slowed his van to a crunching stop as though he had all the time in the world, stepping out onto our unpaved driveway with a broad grin stretched across his sun-worn face.

"I don't know, man. I think women in this town dig the idea that I might be a dirtbag dad," he said in drawn-out syllables, introducing the rental as his "Babe Mobile" while tucking a strand of hair behind his ear. Rivs and I laughed, appreciating the irony: Derrick was, for the moment, married only to the desert and his independence. His baby—a converted live-in 4x4 truck he'd spent years building out—was in the shop for repairs.

After a brief meeting to prepare gear and food, Rivs and Derrick left for the South Rim of the Grand Canyon just before sundown. Rivs often preferred to run the canyon at night—partly to avoid the staggering heat, but mostly to remind himself that he wasn't afraid of the dark.

As an empath, he learned at a young age that sustained movement was the least destructive way for him to metabolize emotional pain—both his own and that which he absorbed from others. He found reprieve from the heaviness only outdoors and through sustained physical exertion.

"I don't run to be fit," he once told me. "I mostly run to not hurt so much."

* * *

I always imagined he left some of his pain at the bottom of the canyon—as though he'd negotiated physical anguish for emotional relief, unburdening himself among the igneous rock and cottonwood trees. Whatever heaviness held him before, he always returned from the canyon a little bit lighter, with gratitude for the life he was able to live and a quiet reverence for the space in which he found it.

This time was different.

When Rivs came home with Derrick the following afternoon, he was shaken. There was a soft fear in his eyes as he hobbled out of the Babe Mobile—the kind that bends inward, imploding in the acknowledgment of one's mortality. I'd seen this look before, just not on him.

"That was rough. I actually thought I might not make it out," he said as he peeled his salt-stained hydration pack out of the trunk.

After a long shower, Rivs laid on the spare mattress we'd put in the basement for Derrick. With eyes half shut he explained his descent down Bright Angel Trail.

He felt short of breath the entire night but tried to brush it off, convinced that his body would sort itself out along the way. It wasn't until fifteen miles into their run—a few miles past Phantom Ranch campground—that Rivs finally stopped running. He was overheating and couldn't keep his heart rate down. He couldn't catch his breath.

"Sorry, man. I think I've gotta cut it short tonight. Something just isn't right," he said, and Derrick agreed in his calm, laid-back manner. Slowly, they started back towards the van rather than continue on to the North Rim of the canyon.

But they only made it another half hour, back to Phantom Ranch, when Rivs said he needed to rest again. Weak and disoriented, he laid himself on an old picnic bench, struggling to breathe.

As a seasoned athlete with an academic background in exercise physiology, Rivs had a good understanding of the human body and how it worked—especially under physical stress. That night, unable to regulate his body temperature and with his heart racing at a rate inconsistent with his fitness, Rivs assumed he was suffering from heat stroke. Even after sundown, the Grand Canyon in June was a quagmire of stagnant heat, with temperatures hovering near 100 around the clock. Tonight was no different, with the Phantom Ranch thermometer reading a stifling 99 degrees Fahrenheit.

By midnight, after spending an hour on the picnic bench sweating through cold chills, Rivs knew that if he didn't get out of the canyon soon, he'd likely die right there beside the Colorado River. Both he and Derrick had spent enough time in dangerous situations to know that the bottom of the Grand Canyon was not a place to be when things weren't going right, especially during a global pandemic. With all national parks closed due to COVID-19—the Grand Canyon included—tonight there would be no park rangers, no mule trains, no helicopters, no rescue teams to call.

Feverish and disoriented, Rivs picked himself up off the bench and forced down a burrito before starting on the five-thousand-foot ascent.

The climb out took ten hours—a stretch of switchback trails that he normally completed in less than two.

"I really didn't think I was gonna make it," he confessed that evening, the two of us squeezed next to Derrick on the mattress. Rivs kept shaking his head in disbelief.

After a takeout meal that he hardly touched, Rivs asked if I'd inflate a blow-up mattress for him in the basement, where it was cold and dark.

He slept for eighteen hours straight, long past Derrick's departure the next morning.

* * *

The basement became a refuge in the days that followed. Rivs's headache and fatigue grew so extreme he found it hard to even make it to the bathroom. Bit by bit I brought down pieces of our home, from Rivs's favorite blanket to snacks he wouldn't eat and even our only TV.

Concerned with usurping medical attention when the state was drowning in COVID-19, he was adamant about not going to the hospital. Instead, he maintained that hospital beds should be left for those who truly needed them. People in far worse situations were being denied emergency treatment, and he didn't want to add to the problem.

He may have been stubborn, but he was not opposed to medical intervention. Nor was he a novice when it came to making accurate diagnoses and triaging patients—skills he had learned in his physical therapy program. During the first week of his illness he went to two urgent care car-side appointments, where he was instructed to go to the ER—which he did not. He did not want to sit in a COVID-19-filled emergency room at the Flagstaff Medical Center, which, at that point, was one of the most overwhelmed medical facilities in the nation.

"I can't go, babe. That's where people go to die right now."

Despite the lethargy, profuse night sweats, splitting headaches, and the occasional blood-stained urine, Rivs assured me that he would just "rest it off." Endurance athletes put their bodies through such duress that illness is quite common in the days following extreme exertion. At least that's what he told me, and I believed him. I always believed him.

In the end we blamed his symptoms on fallout from heat stroke. That is, until his cough started.

* * *

The next morning, I googled "Coronavirus symptoms" as Rivs shivered beside me in the basement. His mom had flown our daughters to her home in Oregon for the beginning of summer break, and I had moved downstairs to be with Rivs while they were away. Landing on one of the thousands of news articles detailing the timeline of COVID-19 symptoms, I scanned the text before reading the words out loud, validating what we had already concluded: Rivs had COVID-19.

"Illness generally presents as fatigue and fever during the first few days of illness, with a severe cough developing on day seven."

He didn't have a fever, but his body was having a hard time regulating its temperature. Despite the Arizonan summer warmth, he was in a constant state of cold sweats.

"I tripped in the canyon and caught COVID," Rivs joked and I laughed along, though he whispered it between bloody coughs while sweating through yet another earth-toned T-shirt.

Later that day he pulled himself out of bed to drive to the pandemic testing site that had been thrown together on county fairgrounds a few miles from our house. Our girls were coming home from Oregon the next day, and we wanted to know if he was contagious before they returned.

He staggered out of the basement, squinting his eyes in the sun he hadn't seen in over a week while lumbering over our feral cat Cici, who always seemed to be curled around his legs. I watched him shake as he stepped into his old Land Rover, his tall and thinning frame bowing uncomfortably while folding himself into the driver's seat. Rivs—the man I'd watched win marathons on the edge of consciousness—was struggling to climb into his car. I almost allowed fear to creep in but instead kept a steady hand on the small of his back until he was sat behind the wheel.

When he came home three hours later, he decided to go for a short run.

"Just to see where I'm at," he reasoned while fighting with his shoe-laces over my delicate insistence that he take it easy instead.

Earlier that year, Rivs had injured himself during the Houston marathon—the last qualifying race for the 2020 Olympic trials, which was an event he had been training for his entire life. After running twenty-three miles below qualifying pace (5:11 minute miles), he made a misstep three miles from the finish line. Landing his foot in a shallow pothole on the periphery of the course, his leg buckled, consequently tearing his hamstring and meniscus. He called me from a bystander's phone as I waited for his victory finish, his voice rife with regret.

"I'm in rough shape, babe. I can't finish. I'm so sorry."

I'm so sorry because barring severe injury, Rivs felt ethically obliged to finish every race he started. *I'm so sorry* because he knew how much time we'd both invested for him to make it to that start line. *I'm so sorry* because he felt there was moral weight to his performance, that our investment was only worthwhile if we cashed in with winning chips. I never saw it that way, but I'd likely made him feel it, as partners sometimes do when balancing the ledger of building dreams and raising children.

Rivs fell into a deep depression in the weeks that followed Houston. Unable to run and with nothing to train for, the culmination of his life dream was shattered as abruptly as his misstep on the marathon course. The emergence of COVID-19 and its quarantine parameters only made him slip deeper into his mind's own darkness. Running was his only refuge, pushing his body through extremes the only way he knew how to sift through it all. Without outdoor movement, Rivs had no way to process his emotions.

"I feel like I'm rotting from the inside," he'd say.

I knew this as I watched from the living room window while he hobbled up our street the afternoon of his COVID-19 test. He struggled across the asphalt, his body lurching forward as he coughed.

He was trying to convince himself he still had miles left in him—that he wasn't as sick as he knew he was. I wasn't in my childhood living room surrounded by siblings but I recognized it all the same: a plea to the grand arbitrator of life and death with whom there is no bartering.

He lasted a few hundred feet up our street before sinking to his knees. He crouched down on the pavement, looking for something to ground him, his legs shaking as he tried to stand over and over again. The scene called me to a distant memory that now felt fresh—a father's head lowered in submission, his eyes searching for a confirmation of health while unwilling to relinquish his once colossal body.

I walked away from the window as he stumbled back home.

* * *

When his test results came back negative the next day, we reassured ourselves with news articles on the fickle reliability of PCR tests and statistics of false negative results. In our minds, COVID-19 was the only possible explanation for Rivs's symptoms. Either that, or he had bacterial pneumonia, perhaps as a consequence of heat stroke.

That evening I gathered our girls from the airport while an ocean of storm clouds stacked up above the San Francisco Peaks. The sun was just disappearing behind the ridgeline, sending broad swaths of pink and orange like watercolors across the monsoon sky. I pulled up to Flagstaff's two-terminal airport to see Harper, Iris, and Poppy splashing in the curbside puddles as Rivs's mom, Julie, stood grinning with a sweatshirt pulled over the top of her head to protect against the rain. And for a moment I could almost convince myself that Rivs wasn't as sick as I knew he was—that I would come home to find him moving his belongings back upstairs with a worn smile on his face. He'd bring us all in for a hug, breathing in deep. "That was a rough one," he'd say.

I stared at my girls playing together in the rain, begging for this to be my reality, my eyes searching for confirmation for it to be true.

But I knew that Rivs was seriously ill. I *knew it*. I had simply never been taught to listen to myself.

Julie offered to stay and help with the girls when I told her that Rivs's condition hadn't improved, though she had a ticket booked for a return flight later that evening.

"I'm sure he'll be fine," I said and she agreed.

"He's one stubborn boy. But yes, I'm sure he'll be fine. Somehow he always is, isn't he?"

That night I told my children that their dad was "just a little sick." I led them to hope's solid ground because I wanted something firm to stand on myself. I shielded them from fear and uncertainty because I wanted to keep them safe. I wanted to keep them innocent. I wanted to keep them happy, as though their happiness was something within my control.

I tucked them into bed high between the branches with the words of my mother.

"Dad is going to be fine. Just fine, my loves."

I hadn't yet learned that we shine the broad spectrum of possibility when we fear the dark cave of probability. I didn't know that the finality of death is a yawning wholeness too deep for some parents to navigate with their children—that facing grief on my own would be achingly different from carrying it along with my children's sorrow. I didn't see how the pain would compound to a suffocating degree, how I would get lost in its darkness so I'd crawl towards the only light I could see.

Hope. Faith. Miracles.

Not trite offerings to soothe fearful kids but a mother's plea that someone save her, too.

I put my girls to bed not knowing how easy it is to blame parents for the things we do not understand. But now I wonder, when my mother offered me hope when I was a child, did she know how sick my father was?

Or had she, too, never been taught to listen to herself?

CHAPTER 4

Born in 1959, Mum was raised in a rundown flat without heat or hot running water on a treeless road in Tottenham, England. Everything about her neighborhood was bleak, from the uniform townhomes lining her street to the grassless front yards hedging their derivative brown brick, row after row.

Growing up, her father worked as an elevator mechanic after spending six years stationed on a WWII warship in East Africa for the British Royal Navy. Her mother, who had been a factory worker since the age of fourteen until she gave birth to Mum's older sister, did her best given the fact that her own mother—an orphaned laundress from East London—had been steeped in alcoholic depression ever since losing two of her four children before they'd reached adolescence. My grandmother was the only surviving child of a mother who had been given away by her parents in infancy, my mum the product of a lineage of women who knew little maternal affection.

Typical of a working-class family in mid-century London, Mum shared a bed with her only sibling, Janet, who was seven years her senior. Their room overlooked the small back garden that their father took great pride in, where he'd grow the sorts of flowers the neighbors said wouldn't thrive without constant sunlight. Despite the dreary climate of North London, each July there would be vibrant blooms of lily of the valley and bougainvillea spilling over their tarred fence, bringing color to an otherwise colorless neighborhood.

Like my mum, my grandad was generally content with whatever life offered and never complained about his circumstances. Every Saturday evening he'd walk Mum down to the public bathhouse with a large metal bucket in one arm and her hand in the other.

Together they would slip into the dingy brick building that reeked of stale bodies and urine while her dad paid the bathhouse fee. Mum held on to her slick bar of soap that dwindled in size each week, careful not to drop it on the concrete floor laced with hair and soiled suds while he filled up their bucket. After scrubbing her body quickly, before the water cooled, Mum would sit in the tub so her dad could wash her tawny hair while humming a sea shanty so loud it made her blush.

Born Anglican but raised agnostic, Mum converted to Mormonism at the age of fourteen when a toll-free number flashed on her TV screen at the end of an episode of *The Osmond Show,* offering the promise of eternal families and god's love. Captivated by Donny Osmond's radiant smile, and decidedly lonely ever since Janet had moved to Turkey three years earlier, Mum called the number on a dreary afternoon in 1973, inviting the Mormon missionaries into her home. Her parents were wary but permitting, and two months later she was baptized into the Church of Jesus Christ of Latter-day Saints.

Joining the church gave Mum the sense of community she longed for. It felt like home. She took the bus to church alone each Sunday wearing the same brown corduroy dress she had sewn on her mother's old Singer. She dreamed of marrying a Mormon man in the temple and building a faithful family of her own, like the ones they taught her about at Sunday school.

One evening at the age of nineteen, while working as a caterer in Alberta, Canada, during her gap year between secondary school and university, my dad showed up for a business event. He was a twenty-six-year-old French-Canadian businessman named Pierre with a broad chest, kind brown eyes, and a smile that lit up the whole room. Mum was swept off her feet that very night.

Dad begged her to marry him a few months later but Mum resisted, trying to preserve her dream of returning to England for nursing school and raising a cohesive Mormon family. Dad was born Catholic, his own mother raised in a convent, but he had rejected religion in his adolescence. He wouldn't convert to Mormonism, he said, but god damnit he promised to love her better than any man ever could. After weeks of debate, entangled in the guilt of faith and perfection so perniciously sold by religion, Mum finally agreed to marry him.

She was still nineteen years old when they were married in Banff, Alberta. Dad used most of his savings to fly Mum's parents out from England—the only guests other than Dad's small family and five close friends. Mum looked beautiful and only a little bit terrified in the eyelet gown she sewed on the machine Dad bought her as an early wedding gift, her long black hair falling thick and straight against her slender frame.

My sister Rachel was born in Calgary less than a year later, shortly after Mum's twentieth birthday. Relinquishing what little sense of self she might have gained by that age, from that day forward everything Mum did was for her children. Though she never once mentioned regret when speaking of motherhood, I sometimes wonder how she felt as a young mother who'd left everything behind: family, homeland, education, the dream of a Mormon family, herself. I wonder if she ever felt cornered into the life that had crept up on her. When she rocked her newborn daughter to sleep, did she lament the life she'd once imagined? Or like so many women entwined in puritanical culture, maybe motherhood came with the denial of herself entirely. Perhaps devotion and family became her new identity. From the moment Rachel was born, perhaps Susan ceased to exist.

Throughout my childhood, I liked being Mormon. Mum took us to church on Sundays and Dad had lunch ready for us when we came home. It was usually takeout, but Mum never uttered a word about breaking the Sabbath when we walked through the door to a bounty of fried chicken displayed on the kitchen table like fine dining. Instead she'd smile as he welcomed us in, his arms stretched out wide, asking "How are my little Mormonites today?" with a broad grin on his face and the smell of KFC wafting through the house as he kissed her long and deep. Their love overrode the normal contentions that often accompanied religious divergence in marriage, to the point where I never even knew it mattered. In the end, he was a man of his word; he never converted to Mormonism, but he loved her better than any man ever could.

Religion was simple back then: catchy songs about obedience, warm cookies handed out after Sunday school, and Mum scratching our backs during the sacrament meeting, where we'd sit in the front pew and draw pictures while members of the congregation spoke about god and his benevolence.

From a young age I was taught that god was a merit-based interventionist—one who would save me from my mortal sins if only I did my part. One who could move mountains and heal the sick so long as I stayed honest, virtuous, and chaste. As a thirteen-year-old confronted with the reality of losing my father, I was counseled by church leaders that a Heavenly Father would hear my earnest pleas if I exercised perfect faith.

And maybe that's not how they said it but that's how I heard it—an impressionable child who hadn't yet learned that the space between sin and perfection was as nebulous as prayer.

Perfect. It was a word passed around church like mints from a cardigan pocket. It was a ladder built on rules whose steps were as slippery as the concept itself. It was a concept handed to me as a crisp offering, belied in goodwill and presented as the ultimate yet unattainable goal, because I was taught that perfection wasn't in the cards for me in this life. That it was only through god I would become what I was intended to be: perfect and whole.

But oh, how I tried.

They didn't see how that word, offered so earnestly, took root in my fertile mind. How it coiled around my tender heart and grew into a shame so deep I didn't even know it had been tilled.

So I reached for it, wanting desperately to believe that perfection was the path to healing my dad, that my obedience could be cultivated into a saving grace. In the innocence of youth, guided by god-fearing words that clamored for exaltation, I believed my dad would live. I knelt by my bedside night after night, my hands clasped together in prayer as I climbed, slipping on faith's mercurial rungs.

I waited for the miracle wide eyed and willing, encouraged by well-meaning church members who offered divine inspiration on his condition, hoping that a projection of faith might cushion the pain of our inevitable reality. Or maybe they truly believed they had received divine revelation on my behalf as they'd hold my hand, saying "I feel prompted to tell you that he will be healed" or "I received confirmation that he will make a miraculous recovery" through tearful eyes. And I devoured their offerings hungrily, desperate for any morsel of hope.

I studied my Book of Mormon with a yellow highlighter, taking note of any passages that spoke of faith and healing. I wrote them down on index cards in bold Sharpie, taping some to my bedroom wall and placing others on Dad's tray table so god could tally the quotes, take note of my devotion, and exert his fickle mercy on my atheist father.

Rachel and Dave had rebelled against the church in their early teens, and at the age of ten, Phil was too young to understand the fragile balance of perfection, faith, and healing. In my mind, it seemed that Dad's miracle was an unspoken responsibility to be shared between Mum and my thirteen-year-old self.

But as my dad deteriorated over the months, the diametric between my prayers and his condition was undeniable. The more I prayed, the worse he became. As his body fell apart, I could no longer reconcile the dissonance between what I'd been taught and what was actually happening to my father.

My prayers were not saving him.

My perfection was not making him whole.

Instead of praising a Heavenly Father for a miraculous healing, I was forced to accept the certitude of my own father's death.

I adopted an existential epistemology: if prayer and faith and god weren't real, then nothing really was. Caught in the rage of nascent grief, I released myself from the dichotomy of black and white with nothing to catch my fall.

Because that's how it is when people lose their faith—when they are taught to believe that morality is only found in gods and rules and religion. Having never established my own barometer of right and wrong, I was left in a diaphony of gray.

Three days after my dad died, I broke a cardinal Mormon rule and got drunk. I slipped on one of Rachel's tube tops and a short pleather skirt and chugged down three lemon-flavored beers at a high school house party with Dave. After making out with a few boys from his eleventh-grade class, I spent the rest of the night crying under a dining room table until he finally coaxed me out.

"Everyone's drunk, Steph. No one's gonna remember you crying," Dave said while walking me home well before his curfew, leaving behind his friends and all the girls fawning over him.

Over the next two years, Mum turned a blind eye to my grief while handling Dad's death without a hint of self-pity. She came to our swim meets, packed our school lunches, and mowed the lawn without complaint. She started working as a nurse's aide for the terminally ill but made sure to be home every afternoon by the time we got home from school. She didn't speak of Dad much, but she never moved on, either. "I'm fine, just fine," she would have said if we had asked, though we never did.

Dad was the love of her life, and that was that.

"How *are* you?"

It was the simplest question we never thought to ask.

But she was visibly gutted when she found a six-pack of beer hiding in my closet when I was sixteen. I had been binge-drinking ever since Dad's death but had somehow managed to hide it from her. That, or she had hidden the truth from herself, unwilling to mourn another wayward child while she mourned the death of her husband.

When she uncovered the beer from beneath a pile of clothes in my room, she was devastated. Unable to deny my rebellion now that the evidence was staring back at her through six lukewarm bottles, that night she met me with an anguish I had only seen in her once before, when she had gripped the metal rails of my father's hospice bed the night he died. And like that night, she stared at me silently before going back to the kitchen, only this time to make stir-fry chicken for dinner rather than to call the coroner.

The myth of my perfection vanished as abruptly as my father's body, covered up and carted away with lifeless finality. Just like that, it was gone.

Looking back, I could say I was upset with my mother for raising me to believe in miracles, but the truth was that she had always given me a choice. She never forced religion on me, like some Mormon mothers did. She let me sit in the parking lot during Young Women's group—a Sunday school class that taught, among other things, the eternal impetus of marriage and motherhood to girls ages twelve to seventeen. She didn't say a word when I wore fishnet tights and an array of facial piercings to church while other girls my age wore modest skirts and floral dresses. She allowed me to move freely in my rebellion with little more than fleeting glimpses of deep disappointment.

No, Mum had never forced miracles or perfection on me. But anger is diffusive. When my sadness was too painful to feel, I reached for the more comfortable emotion. Rage.

That night I wanted her to yell so I could feel justified in my anger. I wanted her to scream in my face, to spew hurtful words she couldn't take back. I wanted a reason to hate her, but the quiet disappointment she offered was solely mine.

"Just leave me the fuck alone. It's *my* life! Why don't you care about something *real*, like the war crimes being committed right now in Afghanistan?!"

I was such a child.

I glanced out the kitchen window as heavy snowflakes blanketed our home. And Mum just stood there, holding the beer in her hands.

I gave her one last look before running out the front door, my feet soaked by wet snow as I hurtled down the driveway wearing nothing but an oversized sweatshirt and black leggings. I wanted to be sure she would worry so I purposefully left my jacket behind.

I wish I had known that all the pain I was carrying, my mother was carrying too. I wish I could have seen that a mother's suffering is always compounded by the pain of her children.

But I was sixteen. I wasn't searching for a martyr. What I needed was someone to blame.

The evergreens bent heavy as I ran down the streets that landscaped my childhood, hedged by innocence, trimmed with faith. Though I knew each curve of pavement like the creases of my father's palm, that night I felt like a stranger, a visitor in my own body, uncomfortable in this puckering skin on the roads I used to call home.

The rage curdling inside me felt dangerous. Flammable, even. I felt the urge to scream but thought I might combust if I let it out. So I kept it in, stifled it, pushed it down like I had been doing for the past two years. It felt safer here, buried inside. I didn't think of my dad once. Instead, I thought about Afghanistan and decided that my anger was a direct result of the Bush administration and the fact that my mother seemed more concerned about beer in my closet than tyrannical bombs being dropped over Kabul. I wondered how she could be so ignorant.

Cocooned in the catharsis of misplaced rage, I ran until I reached a gas station pay phone two miles from my house. The streetlamps were covered in white, sending a hallowed glow over the store where

Dave had bought me beer two years earlier. Somehow in the shrouded light everything looked less severe, as though the pursuit of perfection hadn't ended in this very spot. As if dissension was welcome.

It's softer here, for now.

I picked up the frozen payphone and it stuck to my hand as I dialed a collect call to my boyfriend, Matt, who lived in Tennessee.

* * *

I first met Matt at church, where he was introduced to me as Elder Manning—a twenty-one-year-old Mormon missionary assigned to the Montreal mission, committed to two years of service and celibacy, sharing the restored gospel of Jesus Christ with Southeast Quebec. We had an instant connection despite my resistance to all things Mormon. He was a blue-eyed punk rocker with PUNX tattooed on his knuckles who preached forgiveness and love to our congregation, rather than the usual rhetoric of faith, blessings, and obedience I had grown to despise.

To avoid the potential of forming relationships with members of the opposite sex, missionaries were paired with a companion from whom they could only be separated when bathing or sleeping. They were not permitted to make personal phone calls other than to designated family members twice a year—Mother's Day and Christmas—and were prohibited from being alone in a room with anyone other than their companion. Due to these hardline rules, Mum assumed my friendship with Elder Manning would be stunted in innocent hallway meetings that might leave a lasting impression on my soul.

She was excited that I had a Mormon friend and encouraged our casual interactions. She pretended not to watch from the corner of her eye when we stood in the church corridors talking about music and the abhorrence of capitalism—our bodies leaning closer each week as his companion hovered nearby. What she didn't see was the small black notebook we passed back and forth each Sunday, its contents starting with morbid cartoon sketches that escalated into torrid love notes as the weeks progressed.

When Matt was sent to a new district during a routine missionary transfer, I wondered if I'd ever see him again. Three weeks later he was standing on my doorstep while I was in my bedroom working on an eleventh-grade homework assignment.

Mum called me from downstairs.

"Uh, Steph? Elder Manning is here for you!"

I pulled a leather vest over my black hoodie and ran to the front door.

Matt was standing there wearing blue jeans, a studded leather belt, and a black The Casualties shirt. His head was freshly shaved, straight to the scalp, and there was a duffle bag covered in punk band patches slumped by his feet. I had never seen him wear anything other than a black suit and tie, his designated missionary uniform. Tonight he looked so . . . normal. I threw my arms around him.

It was the first time we had ever touched.

"Hi," he said, pulling back to tell me he loved me right there in the entryway. "I'm leaving my mission to be with you."

"Okay," I whispered with a smile.

Mum maintained that our relationship was innocent and let Matt sleep in Dad's old hospice room that night. Matt and I stood side by side, smiling nervously as she blew up the spare air mattress we kept in the garage for visitors, watching as she wrestled with the pump, because blowing up the mattress was something Dad would have done. If I was more astute to anyone's feelings other than my own, I would have noticed that Matt didn't offer to help. But then again, I didn't, either.

After the bed was inflated, Mum unfolded Dad's tray table and placed a bottle of water on it like you would find in a hotel room.

"There," she said, only a little out of breath. "Now up you get, Steph! You still need to go to school tomorrow. We'll call the mission president in the morning and get this all sorted."

Up I went, but later that night I sneaked back down and laid on top of him with all the seduction a sixteen-year-old could muster.

Matt welcomed me with greedy hands, the months of celibacy obvious in his body as he pulled down my underwear and lunged himself inside me. I let out a subdued yelp and told myself that pain was good as he strangled me.

Matt lived at my house for the next two weeks, until Mum found a used condom in a bathroom trash can and finally accepted that our relationship was anything but innocent. She kicked him out in the dead of night, yelling to grab his things or else she would call the cops and charge him with statutory rape! He left for Tennessee the next day after spending the night in a bus stop shelter, but our relationship continued through letters and phone calls.

* * *

"I hate my mum, Matt. Can you come get me?" I growled into the gas station pay phone when Matt picked up that night, as though he lived down the street and not in another country across a continent. Turned on by my desperation, he said he would take the week off work and leave within a few hours.

I thanked him and said I love you, not knowing where to go after we hung up. I wanted to get drunk, but I had no money and my fake ID was sitting in my wallet at home. Lost and angry I sat on the icy ground with my back against the gas station wall hoping someone might buy me a drink on their way home from work.

It was less than twenty minutes later that a police officer pulled up beside me and motioned me towards him. I could feel the warmth coming from inside his car and imagined hot air blowing from the vents, thawing my fingers and toes. I hesitated as punk rock lyrics about police brutality paraded through my mind.

But I was so cold. I stood and walked towards him.

"Were you looking for me?"

"I was searching for a jacketless teenage girl wandering the streets of Beaconsfield. There aren't many to choose from."

He flashed a smile.

"Your mother is worried about you," he said, motioning for me to sit in the car.

The cold having whittled away what little defiance I had left, I climbed into the front passenger seat, submitting to the fact that I was going home after having been a runaway for less than an hour. I hadn't even earned a ride in the back.

I wanted him to be a dick so I could yell "fuck police brutality" and kick through his window. I wanted him to grope my body so I could scream "pedophile" in his face. More than anything, I wanted justification for my anger. I wanted so badly to be bad. To be reckless. To be defiant. To be as far away from perfect as I could be.

But he was kind.

My eyes welled with tears when I told him that I didn't really know why I ran away.

"I'm just really upset about the war in Afghanistan," I said.

"Well, I can understand the sentiment. But maybe you should try again in the summer—or at least wear a jacket next time," he said as he dropped me off at my house.

I stepped out of the cop car and stood in front of my home as the officer idled in the driveway, waiting to be sure I went inside. The pristine white shutters and baby blue facade welcomed me towards a house that was now unfamiliar. I opened the front door that had both cradled and failed my innocence to find Mum pacing nervously in the entryway hall.

I wish I had known how she was breaking, too.

"You know that I really do love you, Steph."

"I know, Mum. I'm sorry."

I walked past her and climbed the stairs towards my bedroom, passing the sign Phil had hung on my door a week earlier. "When life gives you lemons, make lemonade!" he wrote in purple marker with a collage of lemons in the background. I left it hanging because I only felt fondness for Phil, who used to hide under my bed on lumbar puncture day every other Thursday. "Phil's not here," I'd say to Mum or Dad, trying to protect him as he hid, his steroid-swollen cheeks reddened by heat or maybe fear as he huddled under my quilt. But the time for believing that pain could be shielded by blankets and love was long gone.

I walked past the sign and fell back onto my bed. Tears rolled down my face and pooled in my ears.

Take it easy. Take it easy.

My hands gripped the camouflage quilt Mum had sewn the year Dad was sick, sometime between administering injections, emptying bedpans, and dressing bedsores. From her I learned loyalty and service, but I had never been taught how to be sad. I never knew it was a thing to be learned.

I was surrounded by love—my mother's forgiveness, the sign, the quilt, the kind policeman—and still I felt so lonely. It's a peculiar thing to feel cornered by love when you can't find a source to accept or reciprocate the feeling. The pressure creates a vacuum. It sucks the air from around you and fills the void with shame, leaving you in a state of emotional inertia. That's where I was, crying in silence on my love-adorned bed, marooned in loneliness.

My sadness was a fire, too hot to approach directly so I warmed myself by its rageful flames.

When Matt showed up on my doorstep a few days later, I already had a bag packed. I told Mum where I was going and didn't give her an option to stop me. I spent the next week living in his gutted Honda van, eating McDonald's McChickens for lunch between school classes, drinking forties of beer for dinner at the skate park, and getting lessons in bondage and violent "love" in between, convinced that I had reached the pinnacle of human emotion: rage.

Rage, and shame.

Shame for not saving my brother. Shame for not saving my father. Shame for not being perfect.

And so I burned.

For years to come, rage would direct my every move, catalyzed by the failed expectations of my faith.

In the wake of my father's death, I boxed up faith, hope, and spirituality and labeled them with a strict note to self in the archives of my mind: *Rotten. Do Not Touch.*

CHAPTER 5

Three weeks after Rivs's cough started, I was winding my way towards Humphreys Peak on a pine-lined highway. The bluebird sky gleamed with a crispness found only at high elevation as the thick warmth of early July welcomed me to a day on the western slope of Flagstaff's San Francisco mountain range.

While Rivs's condition deteriorated at home, I was heading to a picnic with my kids, joined by Phil's ex-wife and their three kids. A statuesque beauty with long brown hair, oceanic eyes, and a heart that matched her stunning looks, Tawny and I had remained close after their amicable divorce. With our families' children close in age, we made it a point to meet up every few months—the drive from their home in LA to our place in Flagstaff an easy seven hours through the Mojave Desert. I had made plans to head to LA to let our kids quarantine together—the restlessness of pandemic isolation by now having crawled deep under our skin. But when Rivs's condition hadn't improved as summer creeped on, Tawny rented a small studio to visit us in Flagstaff instead.

Before she arrived, Rivs reassured me that it wouldn't be long before he turned a corner. After a series of telehealth appointments, he had finally convinced a physician to prescribe him azithromycin and dexamethasone, the antibiotic and corticosteroid combination widely used to treat pneumonia and COVID-19 patients. If he *did* have COVID-19— which we assumed he did—then this would be the same treatment he would receive in the hospital. If he *didn't* have COVID-19, he would surely catch it while waiting in an overcrowded ER, which would dangerously complicate whatever lung infection he was battling.

It would only be a few more days until he was better, he said, and I believed him. I believed him even after checking on him the morning of the picnic to find him gasping for air in shallow breaths. I believed him even after he barely opened his eyes and mumbled "'kay" when I told him I'd be back in a few hours.

After all, he was going to turn a corner any day now.

Instead of urging him to the hospital, I made sandwiches, cut up some fruit, and loaded the kids into the car. I gave Tawny instructions on how to find our secret spot burrowed deep on the open glades of Humphreys Peak in case we were separated as she followed behind me. I placed a blueberry smoothie by Rivs's mattress in the basement, dimmed the lights, and left him alone.

My throat was in knots as I backed out the driveway, like I had something important to say but didn't have the courage to say it. Two decades after my father's death, I was still scarred by the idea of inspiration, still revolted by any mention of intuition or "divine" impression, the notion spoiled by the faithful platitudes offered so eagerly by members of my church over the course of his illness.

But truth aches. It is a living creature with a pulse of its own, a caged beast that beats, beats, beats in our chests. A melody playing on repeat, looping over and over until we finally find the strength to listen.

* * *

Six months earlier, a friend encouraged me to do a heroic dose of psilocybin mushrooms. Living adjacent to the Navajo and Hopi cultures of northern Arizona, I was aware that various psychedelics had been used in medicinal and shamanic modalities for centuries in many Indigenous cultures. Intrigued but skeptical about the enlightening effects of entheogens, I had been researching the neurological benefits of psilocybin and was encouraged by a Johns Hopkins study that found astounding results for adults with refractory depression and anxiety. After reading Michael Pollan's book *How to Change Your Mind*, which extended incredible scientific data and personal anecdotes on psychedelics' ability to revive stagnant neuropathways, I committed myself to a "mushroom journey" under the supervision of a plant medicine guide.

In all of my reading on psychedelics, spiritual experiences occurred in an overwhelming majority of cases—80 percent. Considering my tumultuous relationship with spirituality, I believed myself impervious to such transcendentalism. Among other reasons, I was motivated to use psilocybin as a challenge to the construct of god itself.

It was a cold evening in early January when I choked down five grams of psilocybin tea in the living room of my medicine guide's house, nestled deep in a northern Arizona forest.

Less than thirty minutes later, reality began to shift across the plains of perception.

It starts with the Oregon ivy plant sitting on an upright piano, spiraling towards me in a stretch of vibrant green, dancing or maybe growing as its vines pulse to the metronomic beat inside my chest. The plant is a goddess, glistening with intent and far more awareness than I'll ever have. When I walked into the room an hour ago she was a houseplant, vague and unremarkable.

But now I see.

I apologize for not noticing her beauty before—for not appreciating the miracle before me. I run my fingers along the wall as it breathes, in and out, in and out. I trace the crystalline mandalas sparkling on translucent white paint as my fingers sink into the drywall. I look at my hand and wonder where my body ends, and the wall begins.

I try to remember who I used to be, but I am too far from the concept of self. I have forgotten my name, my age, my identity— everything that makes me, me. I am separated from my body, my consciousness scattered across the universe, infinitely fragmented. In an instant I know that I am a minuscule part of an interconnected whole, that individuality is subservient to the universality of existence, that humanity is an eternal tapestry stitched together by love. Through the rips and tunnels of hallucination I am anchored by this transcendent power. As my consciousness scatters like fireflies in the dark, I know that the love I am feeling is some form of god.

It is an astounding discovery, though almost embarrassing in its simplicity: we are all connected in love.

Time, space, birth, death, human, god, love, pain—all of these things are moving parts twisting through the universe—not separate or linear but bending pieces of a unified whole. It is an epiphany that shakes me from a deep sleep, and I see that existence is both beautiful and terrible all at once. In order to appreciate the breadth of life, I know I have to accept these two truths as equally important: beauty and terror.

It is euphoria and horror as I swim through the cosmos. I don't know whether I want to escape or feel this way forever. My ego stripped bare, I feel both mortally insignificant and universally loved in the inexorable macrocosm of existence, a now-revived relic of unending impermanence.

Overwhelmed by the experience of everything, I let the medicine guide take my hand and lay me down on a nest of blankets next to a crackling wood stove. I hear the synapses firing in my brain, like an explosion of atoms through eternity.

I close my eyes and travel through the technicolored conduits of awareness that flash through my mind. Through it all, despite the fear and disorientation, I feel another truth budding in my chest: nothing matters but love.

After minutes that feel like years of lying next to the fire, I remember that I do have a human body, though now it feels as though I am floating away from it. Panicked by the disconnect, I open my eyes and look for the medicine guide to ground me.

"It's all just too much," I say.

Her face shines in harlequin light that shifts as she holds my hand.

"What is too much?" she asks.

"Feeling it all," I say.

Caressing my back she tells me to breathe, to marvel at the miracle of each inhale as she sits me upright. "It's okay to feel it all," she says.

Though my hands sink into the ground as I try to stabilize myself, I feel anchored by her touch, by our shared humanity.

What a gift to be alive. What a gift to be human. What a gift to be loved.

This wisdom feels more like a memory than a revelation—something I've always known to be true. If nothing else, it is undeniable that my prior grip on reality has been a limited understanding of a larger, perhaps infinite whole. In flashes of vibrancy I see that there is so much more to life than the tangible, that truth is far more complex than the empirical before me. I have always prided myself on intellect, on making conclusions based on verifiable facts. But here I am, traveling through an indemonstrable reality that feels truer than anything I've ever experienced. Rather than feel like a stranger in this new land of bending walls and crystalline mandalas, somehow I am home.

Four hours later, as I come down feeling more loved than I've ever felt, I hear one last resounding message: Trust yourself. All the power you'll ever need is inside you.

I left the medicine guide's house the next morning feeling liberated from my logical mind. I tried to rationalize my experience, but I knew that something deep within me had been reawakened that night.

It wasn't a rebirth. It was an excavation.

My experience gave new meaning to Alan Watts's philosophy—words I'd read before but had never truly understood before experiencing them.

"When you get free from certain fixed concepts of the way the world is, you find it is far more subtle, and far more miraculous, than you thought it was. . . . Only words and conventions can isolate us from the entirely undefinable something which is everything."

That night I became aware of the everythingness of existence while recognizing the extent of love's transcendent power. More importantly, I was starting to entertain the idea that perhaps love was not something to be searched for. Perhaps, instead, it was something that already lived inside me.

I recalled a memory of this power halfway to the picnic with Tawny. Emboldened by the imminence of its timely importance, the truth could no longer be subdued. Finally, it had thrashed its way out. Its presence was so clear that I almost slammed on my breaks as I drove down the thicketed Route 180 towards Flagstaff's dormant volcanic peaks.

I felt it more than I heard it. It was an intuitive knowing—a memory I finally had the courage to remember.

Go home and check on Rivs.

I hesitated for a moment, skeptical of the feeling. But it was the truest thing I'd ever known. I couldn't rationalize it away.

Go home and check on Rivs.

I pulled off the sleepy highway and into a gas station, motioning out my window for Tawny to follow behind me.

"I know this sounds weird, but I think I need to go back and check on Rivs. I'm so sorry, Tawny. Can you take the kids?"

Tawny wrapped me in a warm embrace, cradling the back of my head with her palm. "It doesn't sound weird at all, Steph," she said before loading my kids into her car. "Go. Hurry. I've got you."

"Rivs is going to make fun of me," I thought as I raced home, reminded of my attempted Costa Rica rescue over a decade ago. Laughing nervously at the memory, I tried calling his phone three times, expecting to hear his voice and giggle together about another one of my overreactions.

But the line just kept ringing.

Twenty minutes later, I burst through the basement door to find Rivs lying on his side in bed with a circle of blood pooled around his mouth. I switched on the lights and watched as choppy breaths shifted his body on the mattress. As I approached him, I saw that his lips were tinged blue, his skin unnaturally pale. The sight was all too familiar, and my reaction was more instinctual than pragmatic as decades-old images flooded my mind, unlocking a stunted trauma and rage.

I ran to him and shook his shoulders. "Fuck you, motherfucker, fuck you. No. No. No."

After several desperate jolts he finally opened his eyes and let out a feeble moan.

"You need to go to the hospital, Rivs," I whimpered. Or had I screamed it?

When he shook his head no, I reached for my phone to call an ambulance. He slumped off the mattress and proceeded to army crawl to the bathroom.

"Put th'phone down. I'mmfine . . . see?" he mumbled, hoisting himself up with his hands on the bathroom sink before falling back to the ground.

"*You stubborn motherfucker,*" I thought as I stood in the bathroom doorway.

"I'm calling an ambulance," I threatened. I *still* believed him.

"I won't gedd-in," he snarled, crawling back to the mattress before turning his back to me and shutting his eyes. I would have been offended by his callous defiance, but his behavior was so far from usual that I knew it was a result of illness. Despite his stubbornness, Rivs was soft and kind.

After an hour of slurred debate while drifting in and out of consciousness, he finally agreed to let me drive him to the hospital, motivated by a pulse oximeter that flashed a terrifying 71 percent. We'd purchased the Pulse Ox three years earlier when, at nine months old, Poppy had endured a bout of reactive airways disease. Even in the haze of hypoxia, Rivs understood that a blood oxygen reading under 90 percent was considered a medical emergency.

"Fine, but I'm takin' a shower first," he lobbied, and I agreed, satisfied to have at least coerced his compliance.

With nearly his entire body weight leaned on my frame, together we climbed the fourteen steps to our upstairs bathroom. Gasping for air, he sat on the toilet as I helped him strip off a sweat-soaked T-shirt exposing his protruding spine and spidering ribcage. Under normal circumstances, Rivs would have been proud to finally look like a distance runner.

I shook my head at the thought as he climbed into the shower and waved me away.

I retreated to our bedroom and began stuffing his clothes into a duffel bag for a possible overnight hospital stay. It was only a few seconds later that I heard a sickening thud from the shower.

I dropped a wad of boxer briefs and burst through the door to find Rivs sprawled across the bathroom floor with his torso hanging out of the tub.

Almost instinctively, I ran to Poppy's bedroom and grabbed the oxygen tank that we'd been issued during her sick days three years earlier. Fumbling nervously with the tubing, I carried the tank to Rivs's side, securing the infant nasal cannula to his nose and cranking the oxygen to full blast.

"Fuckyou I'm notgoooooing," he yelled while struggling to shift his body back into the tub, words completely uncharacteristic coming from him. I would later learn that the specific reason for his irrational behavior was a side effect of carbon dioxide poisoning. Rivs's lungs were so sick that his body was unable to pump enough oxygen through his bloodstream to his brain.

In other words, Rivs was slowly suffocating.

I helped him to our bed and threw a pair of underwear on his lap, ordering him to get dressed. There was no more time for timidity, no more bowing to his hypoxic irritability. After running through a checklist of hospital essentials, I led him down to the driveway, his newly slender frame stumbling against the walls on our way to the car.

His consciousness waxed and waned on the twenty-minute drive to the hospital, where he'd wake sporadically to ask, "where are we going?" and respond with a defeated "fuuuuuuuck" each time I told him we were headed to the ER.

It was early evening when we finally reached the Flagstaff hospital, having taken over three hours to convince him of his need for medical care. The dark city sky was studded with stars as I shifted into the emergency department's last available spot, the stillness of a stormless summer night mocking the chaos around us.

"You ready?" I asked, reaching for his hand as my eyes welled with tears. My adrenaline had calmed, and the gravity of our situation was finally sinking in: Rivs was very sick. Due to COVID-19 restrictions, I wouldn't be able to wait with him in the ER. I wouldn't be able to visit him if he was hospitalized. For the first time I realized that it might be days before I saw him again.

"I'mma be okay. Promise," Rivs said, softened by my sadness. "Always am. They can't kill me."

After helping him from the passenger seat, we walked to the emergency reception while Rivs swayed around and I tried to steady his steps. A nurse in blue hazmat gear met us at the entrance of the hospital and told us to wait outside the sliding glass doors. She motioned for him to sit in the last available seat and, observing his general disorientation, called for wheelchair assistance.

My voice trembled as I gave her a rundown of his condition, feeling relieved but terrified while verbalizing his symptoms for the first time: shortness of breath, weakness, oxygen saturation in the low seventies, disorientation, delusions, coughing up blood, lethargy, night sweats, weight loss . . .

The nurse barely looked up from her computer as she typed his information, drained from an endless barrage of patients with similar ailments flooding into the overcrowded and understaffed hospital.

Rivs was drowning on dry land, and so was she.

The nurse finished her notes then led him to the wheelchair, kindly informing me that this is where we'd say goodbye.

As he sat, I leaned down to give him a rushed kiss on the cheek. I didn't want to usurp anyone's precious time given the pandemic's strenuous circumstances.

"Love you, Rivs," I said.

"Lov'you too, Steph," he said as I turned and walked away.

But if I had known.

If I had known, I would have remembered to hold him a little longer. I would have felt him a bit more. I would have listened more intently to how he said my name. I would have rolled the sound around—let it linger.

I would have been more perceptive to the lesson I had been ignoring my whole life: that all of existence is found here, in each breath.

Now I know that truth is extended to us over and over before it is fully understood. Sometimes it takes a bending of tragedy, time, and space before we can love what's before us.

Sometimes we need to run away—from ourselves, from our pain, from our grief—before we can find our way back home.

And run, I did.

CHAPTER 6

After spending a week together in his van, Matt dropped me off at home on a Sunday morning and left for the long drive back to Tennessee.

I walked through the front door to find Mum sitting at the kitchen table, reading her Book of Mormon. I studied her for a moment, almost as intently as she was studying her scriptures. She was beautiful—tall and slim, with chestnut hair that swept her collarbone and silken skin that made her look put together despite her apathy towards fashion and makeup. Her eyes were deep brown and, though tired, they showed no hint of self-pity for the difficult life she had endured.

"Oh, Steph," she said as I walked towards her, offering to wash the dirty clothes from my backpack with a half-cracked smile. I handed them to her with a shame that felt just as soiled and mumbled an apology while climbing the stairs to my bedroom.

It was only a few months later, when I was seventeen, that she decided it would be best if I went to live in Los Angeles with Rachel, who had recently moved there with her actor boyfriend. Eager to leave my home that was mired in memories of the faithful child I wanted to forget, I registered for community college in LA and lived out my last few months in Montreal.

When Mum walked me into the airport for my flight to California, she rambled through a checklist she'd scribbled on scratch paper the night before, calling out each item in such a way that you could tell the list was memorized.

"Socks?! Passport?! Wallet?!"

Mum's nervousness made something crack inside me. If only for a moment, I saw a glimpse of her, a loving mother trying to tenure my pain.

"I'll be okay, Mum. Rachel will take care of me."

"Call me," she said, or maybe pleaded.

I nodded, leaning in to let her give me a quick hug before turning towards the security line. I didn't look back to see if she was crying, to wonder whether she was grieving yet another early loss.

* * *

In the aftermath of Dad's death, Rachel had recommitted herself to Mormonism. Not long after I arrived in LA, she asked me to go to church with her. My first Sunday there, I met the bishop's son and accepted his invitation to a Mormon house party later that week. Considering Mormonism's rigid rules against alcohol, I assumed the party might include a few board games and maybe a couple cans of soda. That Friday I showed up in the most modest apparel I could find—a pair of black Dickies and a Rise Against T-Shirt with ripped sleeves. The bishop's son greeted me at the door with a frosty beer, saying "I could smell crazy on you when I met you!" as though grief was some type of perfume. I smiled and grabbed the bottle from his hand, gulping it down right there in the doorway. Later that night I was making out with him and his girlfriend in the shower while his friends took pictures, gawking and laughing at the spectacle I'd made of myself.

The next morning I decided that I would never go to church with Rachel ever again.

A month later, bored and lonely in a new city that was already tainted by shame and regret, I found myself at an AA meeting with a guy I'd just met after we bumped into each other in the Manic Panic hair dye aisle at Hot Topic.

Andy was a strung-out punk rocker with a kind smile and tattoos up to his chin. He had recently been released from an eighteen-month sentence in the LA county jail for possession of heroin and grand theft auto. As part of his release conditions, he'd received a court order to a halfway house that enforced twice-daily AA meetings.

Proud to look like the reckless teen I was so desperately trying to become, I had simply nodded when he asked if I was an addict and nodded again when he asked if I wanted to get sober. The truth was, the only drug I'd ever tried was weed, which I'd smoked once with Dave when I was fourteen and then spent four hours staring at my reflection in the mirror trying to convince myself that I wasn't *actually* dying.

Andy didn't seem to notice my eyes shifting nervously with my dishonest response, and soon we were skateboarding together down the streets of North Hollywood towards a small church on the corner of Vineland and Camarillo.

Sweating under the scorching sun, we stopped in front of a small building with a sign on its front lawn that read "JESUS LOVES YOU" in bold font. I wondered if they ever changed the sign as he led me past a plastic table lined with doughnuts and coffee and surrounded by an intimidating number of strangers. I was relieved when he pointed me to one of the folding metal chairs set up in neat rows in front of a small wooden pulpit.

"My friend Alberto is sharing today. He's great. I'll introduce you to him after the meeting," he said as the room began filling with people sipping coffee from Styrofoam cups, congratulating each other for their efforts—for simply showing up.

Here it seemed, you came as you were. If nothing else, that was enough, to be you. I settled into my chair, feeling at ease in such a foreign context, comforted by the absence of perfect.

When Alberto approached the podium, he looked much different than I had imagined. Short, thick, and somewhere in his mid-thirties, he greeted the small crowd wearing designer jeans, a red V-neck T-shirt, and a Von Dutch trucker hat. His hair was dark and wavy and fell softly against his bronzed face. He giggled as he lowered the microphone to his mouth.

With candor, Alberto shared his story of addiction, starting with his experience of childhood sexual abuse. By the age of thirteen, he had run away from home in Chicago, funding his way across the country with sex work—a job often assisted by drug use. By sixteen, he was HIV positive and addicted to crack. Apathetic to whether he lived or died, he continued to drift across the country before making a home beside a green dumpster on skid row in downtown LA.

He was seventeen when he was approached by Karen, a social worker pursuing her PhD in the study of child prostitution. Karen was warm and kind, and Alberto trusted her immediately. That afternoon he agreed to go with her to Van Nuys, where she was heading an NGO that aimed to rehabilitate young sex workers.

Alberto would continue to struggle with addiction throughout the years, but after meeting Karen, he never returned to sex work. He finished his story by proudly declaring eight years of sobriety at the age of thirty-three.

"More than anything, I feel blessed to be alive and I'm grateful for each and every day I get to be here with all you beautiful people," he said before doing a curtsy and returning to his seat.

As the crowd erupted in applause, I was overcome by the unquiet itch of self-awareness. Contrasted against Alberto's humble gratitude, I recognized the pettiness of my indignation. Alberto had never felt the earnest embrace of a loving father or experienced the unconditional acceptance of a kind mother. The world had mostly shown him cruelty, and still he chose to see the good in his life.

As I stood to chant "keep coming back, it works if you work it!" with feigned familiarity, I felt a crack in the narrative I had been telling myself—that I was alone, forgotten, used up.

All I'd known was love my whole life. Where was *my* gratitude?

I walked out of the church with a pit in my stomach, uncomfortably aware of myself. That's when I first saw Dylan.

I noticed him from the corner of my eye as Andy introduced me to Alberto, watching as he casually rolled a cigarette from a pouch of Bugler tobacco. He stood with his shoulders hunched forward looking uncomfortable in his body, but he was tall, and I could tell that he had probably once been muscular. He had an angular face with a strong chin and high cheekbones that were even more defined as he took his first drag.

As it turned out, Alberto was Dylan's AA sponsor—someone with extended sobriety who offered encouragement and guidance to those newer to being sober. After a brief introduction outside the church, from that afternoon forward Dylan and I spent nearly every day together. At the age of twenty-three, Dylan had been sober for ninety days when we met, with a history of addiction to meth and crack. After living out of the trunk of his '87 Volvo, Dylan had recently moved from a sober living house and into a small bungalow that sat next to a liquor store in Studio City. Other than the flashing yellow "BEER" sign that mocked him on a daily basis, Dylan was grateful for his small room and the twin-sized bed that he would soon start sharing with me.

I let Matt down with a late-night phone call, telling him we should see other people. He took it hard, telling me to go fuck myself. Two years later, Matt would send me a series of scathing emails stating that I would burn in hell when I met god. Even back then, the irony of his message was not lost on me. "Mormons don't believe in hell, asshole" I had wanted to respond, but never did.

Unlike Matt, Dylan was kind and gentle. Our relationship was my first experience with pure love and romantic affection, a stark contrast against Matt's obsession with dominance and control. Still, it took three weeks for me to build the courage to tell him that I was not an alcoholic or addict. When I told him the truth, he just laughed it off.

Committed to saving the man I had come to love, I got sober with Dylan. We spent our days longboarding down the Venice Beach Boardwalk and hiking through the Hollywood canyon trails, staying busy outdoors to stave off the powerful allure of intoxication. We spent our evenings in AA and our nights holed up in his small bedroom watching movies on the twelve-inch Panasonic TV we found dumpster diving behind Goodwill.

But six months into our relationship, after two hundred and seventy days of sobriety, Dylan said he was in control and wanted to have a beer with me.

"I can handle a drink, Steph," he said, because he thought it was true, wanting desperately to have been changed by my love, and I agreed, hungry myself for love's atoning power.

Later that evening we bought a six-pack of Corona from the liquor store by his house, saying that we'd start slow and not get carried away. After all, we weren't looking to get drunk. Three light beers seemed like a normal amount of alcohol, as though the sentience of pain was quantifiable.

We sat on Dylan's bed with the six-pack nested on the floor, the cold bottles sweating from heat, though I could have sworn it was nerves sending heavy beads down the glass. We sat there for a considerable amount of time, giving ourselves one last opportunity to sway. Perhaps it was a formality to spend the last few moments of his sobriety in reverence, silently eulogizing the end of it.

"Well, we don't want to drink warm beer," he finally said, reaching for the bottles and making a toast *to moderation!*

We finished the six-pack telling a joke here and there to remind ourselves that we were participating in a normal activity. Then the beer was gone and we were left sitting in his small room with nowhere to go and nothing to show for ourselves but six empty slots in a yellow cardboard box.

Suddenly the night was anticlimactic, ending abruptly with one last greedy gulp. By then we had no intention of rationalizing the rest of our night, so we went back to the liquor store and bought a fifth of cheap vodka. Having outgrown Dylan's room with its memories of sobriety, we headed to the Los Angeles River and drank the vodka ravenously, far from the respect we'd given the Coronas.

There was no more homage to be paid to asceticism, no more talk of moderation. Overcome with the brawny freedom of recklessness, we ran up and down the slopes of the Los Angeles River, hollering into the night.

So *free*. So *normal*.

It was only an hour later that Dylan was calling an old friend to buy an ounce of weed. When his friend pulled up to the river, Dylan and I were both drunk enough to forgo the balance of will and temptation, guilt and liberation. Dylan's mind was already committed, and I was too drunk to say anything.

I welcomed his friend with a sloppy hug. A vestige of Dylan's former life, his presence made me feel less responsible for this sojourn from sobriety, and I was happy to hand over the reins of blame.

With my back slumped against the river wall I sat and listened to them talk about the good old days, reminiscing as people do when they have little in common other than a mutual love for getting fucked up.

The thought made me feel lonely and I rose to my feet, steadying my body against the cement riverbank before turning to leave.

"Hey, baby, where are you going?" Dylan asked as a plume of thick smoke leaked out of his mouth, obscuring my view of his face. I was sure there was a metaphor to be found in the imagery but I was too drunk to find it.

"I'm just ready to go home," I said, uncomfortable with the sudden realization that all of Dylan's sobriety chips were being cashed in with me tonight. Or was it because of me? Perhaps he was back down to zero because of our mutual love of getting fucked up.

I took him to an AA meeting the next day because it felt like the right thing to do. He cried into my chest as I stroked his head, my eighteen-year-old hands trying to save a whole man when they couldn't even save me. Friends and strangers approached us, telling us to take it one day at a time and to not be so hard on ourselves. We ate doughnuts off white napkins and drank coffee from Styrofoam cups and chanted "keep coming back; it works if you work it!"

But we kept drinking together, and after a while it *did* start to feel normal. LA's warm Santa Ana winds had wrapped around our bodies like an underhanded embrace, thawing the numbness of contentment that had kept us paralyzed for months. Somehow, we were both most alive in our pain.

Then one night Dylan smoked crack while I was spending two weeks in Montreal, when Alberto showed up at his door with a bag of white rocks, having just learned that he had terminal stomach cancer. Denuded by the months of drinking with me, Dylan quickly gave in to Alberto's plea for an accomplice.

There was no more pretending that addiction was fleeting.

My love couldn't save him.

The next few months were devoted to Dylan's sobriety, where he'd get two days, then a week, then three weeks, then back down to zero and we'd start all over again, sobbing in brown buildings and holding hands with strangers who wished us well.

Like the volatility of sobriety, our relationship grew increasingly tenuous, the sharpness of our decisions a pointed arrow we couldn't escape.

Shrouded in a grief I wasn't ready to acknowledge, I was blind to a truth too bright to see directly: I thought Dylan's love would save me, too.

But something changed the night we shared those Coronas, the sweating bottles holding what neither of us could accept: that all the love in the world can't mend a heart unable to love itself, that normalcy holds no weight in the land of abandoned sons and fatherless daughters.

I would struggle with this reckoning for years to come. Rather than build a home within myself, I continued to search for it in other people, holding partners to the impossible standard of filling the implacable hole left by my father's death.

I didn't know that the gulf of my grief was a passage I would have to navigate on my own. In trying to avoid sorrow, I left myself behind over and over again.

Now I wonder, in the conquest to soothe my pain, how many had I drowned with the leaden belief that I was savable? How many had come up for breath in the airless inadequacy of my grief?

Because my brokenness was not a strait to be crossed or land to be conquered but a sovereign inheritance of my own. Something I would have to accept in order to move forward.

To meet ourselves in the inexorability of grief, that is healing. To understand that strength is moving forward with all of our broken pieces, that is freedom.

CHAPTER 7

The evening Rivs was wheeled into the ER, I felt a hollowness—a separation far more isolating than physical distance. For the first time in our twelve years of marriage, the space between us felt uncompromising.

Weren't you just right here?

Rivs and I were twenty-two when we met. Our life together was built on the painstaking labor of young love, evolving expectations, and a cycle of collaborative new beginnings. I always looked to him for strength, especially in times of hardship. I believed that I *needed* him, that my own power came through him and our union because of what I had been taught, that it was only through god and with a man that I would be complete. That by myself I would never become what I was created to be.

Perfect and whole.

Who was I without him? What was home if not us?

I turned from the hospital and walked back to the car, the night a haunting bleakness despite a brilliant display of stars. Strange, how pain can obscure what's in front of us, like a lens we don't even know we're looking through. In its distortion, everything feels incurably dark.

Over the years, between Rivs's long training hours, my writing ambitions, and our respective grad school endeavors, we had grown accustomed to being apart. Soon after Iris was born, Rivs was hired by a production company, which required him to go overseas several times a year, sometimes in two-week stretches. At first these jobs were sporadic opportunities, but they soon became our primary source of income—much more lucrative than sponsorships, race winnings, or work as a physical therapist. Eventually the payouts from his work trips allowed me to step away from serving tables and focus more on my writing career. I was also able to stay home with our kids in their baby and toddler years, which, it turns out, was what I wanted to do more than anything else.

When Rivs and I were apart, I started to consider the ways I relied on him in situations I could handle on my own. I regained some of the independence I had lost between young marriage and raising children. I grew comfortable being alone and Rivs encouraged my independence. He urged me to travel and write between his work trips, to reestablish the sense of self I had relinquished in early motherhood. Although we struggled to get it right and we were a far-from-perfect couple, in many ways distance allowed our marriage to maintain the autonomy and longing that is sometimes lost in more traditional partnerships.

But as I drove home from the hospital that evening, I felt the harsh difference between loneliness and being alone. Despite our worn-in physical separation, I always had the default of knowing that Rivs was just a phone call away.

Now, I felt the loneliness of his absence. He was just across town, but there were oceans between us. I had been here before and knew what it meant: there would be no assurances extended across the void, no softly mouthed words telling me to "take it easy."

There was no more deferring to his strength.

What I hadn't yet realized is that throughout the course of our marriage, I had been expecting him to validate my broken pieces—to fix what had been fractured by my father's death. This unspoken expectation was an untenable demand, and one I didn't even know I had made. It all came out as projections of deficiency on his part. Over and over I blamed him for my pain when his love couldn't save me.

When he failed to make me whole.

Rivs's hospitalization forced me to recognize a truth I had been avoiding: I didn't know how to be alone.

When he called from the ICU several hours later, he spoke to me in looping metaphor—confused as to where he was and why. High-flow oxygen had lifted him out of hypoxia, but he was now on a slew of painkillers and sedatives, which further distorted his reality and demeanor.

In a meandering conversation sustained by the static of forced air, I gathered that a chest X-ray had found "innumerable" nodules in his lungs. The doctors were unsure what had caused these lesions, which made a medical plan of action difficult, if not impossible. Assuming he had COVID-19, the medical team would need to wait for a positive test result before treating him. In the meantime, they administered the same antibiotic and corticosteroid combination Rivs had given himself at home—only intravenously and in higher doses. Without a diagnosis, all they could do was nurse his symptoms and treat him for a general lung injury.

When I told our girls that their dad was in the hospital, they responded with love and apathy. Our children were accustomed to having a resilient father in extreme circumstances from which he always returned.

My heart broke with their familiar response. I knew the feeling well.

*　*　*

The first week of his hospitalization was a blur of unanswered questions. Rivs was on a cocktail of heavy narcotics and couldn't fully understand what was happening—a disturbing occurrence for someone so attuned to his body. He spent most of the day asleep and would often doze off or lose consciousness mid-sentence whenever we talked on the phone. Other than a CT scan showing thousands of unexplained pulmonary masses and a decimated blood platelet count, no one knew what was wrong with him. Even after three negative in-hospital COVID-19 tests, the leading medical theory was that he'd been infected by an undecipherable strain of coronavirus—the same theory Rivs had believed all along.

"Undiagnosed pneumatological infection or injury. COVID-19 negative. Stable and oriented on four liters of high-flow oxygen," the nurse read from a computer screen each time I called for a synopsis of his condition.

"But this is my husband," I wanted to shout. "He's not just another statistic."

I had watched the COVID-19 body count tick upward on the news, but I was only now coming to understand the depths of its tragedy—a personalization of the individual pain that constitutes a global pandemic. For the first time, I felt a humanization of the worldwide trauma before me.

I could no longer complain about fickle quarantine rules or stressful school closures once I felt the heartbreaking reality of having a loved one suffering alone in the ICU.

Sometimes the universality of pain is recognized only after we experience it for ourselves. Knowing I'd only scratched the surface, I wondered how far I'd been alienated from the depths of human suffering, how heavily I had been blinded by my own privileged perceptions.

Perhaps this was the purpose of a broken heart, to be fractured enough to feel it all. Maybe pain was myopic only when I failed to acknowledge all the love waiting to shelter it.

* * *

During that first week, time crawled forward while my heart was both broken and opened at once. I had never experienced such pain, and at the same time, I had never felt so much love for the world. I had been stripped bare; my armored layers peeled back to the fragility of human existence.

And I lived there, in the thick of universal agony with a deep love for it all, until eight days after his admission. That morning, there was a gutting variation to the nurse's daily update.

"Undiagnosed pneumatological infection or injury. COVID-19 negative. Stable and oriented on max high-flow oxygen . . . Acute right pneumothorax."

The day before, a surgeon had performed a fine-needle lung biopsy to determine the origins of Rivs's lesions. In my recent research on lung disease, I learned that pneumothorax, or a collapsed lung, was a potential side effect of a pulmonary biopsy. I had prepared myself for this possibility prior to the procedure, but because it was *Rivs*, I assumed he'd avoid any complications.

Trying to compose myself—because that's how I thought the wife of a critically-ill partner should be, *composed*—I asked the nurse if I could speak to Rivs directly. Most days I waited for him to call me first, partly to avoid the risk of waking him, but mainly because I was terrified of the endless ringing that often went unanswered.

This time, I heard the harsh roar of oxygen as he fumbled to pick up the phone. His voice was a rush of fabricated breath.

"It's bad, babe. I've got this tube sticking out my chest. I feel like I'm being waterboarded. I can't take a deep breath. They put this mask on me but there's still not enough air in my lungs. I can't get enough oxygen. I can't breathe. Steph. I don't think I'm going to make it."

Click. Silence. Loneliness.

Oxygen. Lungs. Breath.

These words held memories cloaked in a sadness so thick I could barely see straight. Even more frightening was the fact that I had never heard Rivs panic before. Ever.

With a collapsed lung and a tube in his pleural cavity to drain fluid from his chest, the severity of Rivs's illness was finally sinking in.

That night I cried while putting six-year-old Iris to bed, the second verse of her favorite lullaby breaking the composure I was trying to maintain.

The other night dear
as I lay sleeping
I dreamt I held you in my arms

I finished the song between stifled sobs, my fists clenched around Iris's blanket as though brute force could obstruct the flow of tears. By example of my stoic mother, I had learned that parents are meant to bridle their emotions in front of their children. After all these years I still thought that sadness was absolvable. Like prayer, I believed emotions to be exigent offerings into the cosmos, that with enough intention, pain could dissipate into ether.

But suppressed feelings are more like perfection. They fester and rot long before we realize the damage they've done.

The moon was a crescent behind slatted blinds as I staggered out of Iris's bed and into Harper's room, where she was molding clay figurines on her floor. With her knowing eyes, angular face, and freckled nose, she looked just like her father. At the age of ten she had just begun to border the line between childhood and adolescence, her lean frame already filling out in womanly ways that made her feel like a stranger in her own body.

"Hey, Mom! Look at this frog I made!" she said, lifting her creation in an offering of innocence while her eyes shone with venerable pain. Her eyes, they were Rivs's incarnate. They were windows to an old soul that knew sorrow long before experiencing much of her own. Like him, Harper had been born cracked wide open, gifted or perhaps cursed with the ability to recognize and understand the depths of human suffering. Like him, she came into this world feeling it all.

"Amazing, sweetheart. I love it," I managed to say as I knelt beside her and lowered my head.

Sensing my sadness, Harper pulled me in. I leaned into her feeling like both mother and child, the two of us suspended between naivete and knowing as she cradled me in her lap.

I sobbed as she stroked my hair with an empathy far beyond this lifetime. I let myself unravel as she held me close and whispered, "it's okay, it's okay, it's okay."

(Take it easy. Take it easy.)

I left her room that night wondering if I'd ever forgive myself for putting that kind of responsibility on my child when it was enough to break me now, holding someone else's sadness, thinking I could carry it all.

It was something I'd never seen my own mother do—break down, show sadness—even when Dad became delirious and started welcoming us as dinner guests whenever we came in through the front door.

"I'm not your guest! I'm your fucking daughter!" I want to scream, but Mum simply smiles and takes his boney hand in hers, letting him give her a tour of the house they've lived in together for two decades. She nods when Dad points out his favorite La-Z-Boy chair and acts surprised when he gushes about the vintage baby grand piano that his father used to play in jazz concerts.

"I should really learn to play one day," Dad says, running his hand through phantom hair that fell out long ago while Mum glances back at me and giggles, her reaction exaggerated by the relief of a husband standing on his own two feet.

And I stand there beaming, ecstatic to see a smile on her face, not realizing how desperately I am trying to hold her sadness.

Rivs phoned the next morning with no recollection of the panicked call he had made the previous day. Offering the latest hypothesis for his illness while I was cooking breakfast for the kids, he said that the physicians' latest theory was that he had been infected with the bubonic plague while running in the Grand Canyon.

"Okay, but is there *any way* you or someone you were running with stepped on a gopher carcass, causing a gaseous release from its lungs? And if so, is it *possible* that you may have inhaled the contents of said gopher's lungs, thereby breathing in fumes contaminated by bubonic plague?"

His comedic impersonation of the infectious disease specialist made me laugh so hard I almost dropped a pan of eggs on the floor, my reaction exaggerated by the relief of a husband lucid enough for humor. I wasn't sure what had caused his newfound clarity, but I didn't care. Even though he gasped for breath between each few words, Rivs was *here*. And just like that, *I* was back. In his presence, I was whole again.

Trying to regain my composure, I noticed Harper staring at me from the kitchen table, grinning.

The smile on her face was a casting and crumbling. It was a look that spoke of carrying a pain that was not her own, and the weight of that impossible burden. It was a smile that taught me the truth of suffering right there on the kitchen floor: sadness itself is never held, only the space for it.

I scooped eggs from the frying pan and onto three plates, desperate to tell my daughters that my sadness was not theirs to carry. Desperate to let them know that holding me would always be enough.

I wanted them to see that falling apart was a healthy response to trauma. I wanted them to understand that strength is found in buried faces, in the acceptance of hearts cracked open and allowing both light and darkness to gleam through the slats.

I wanted them to know that brokenness was not a war but a surrender, something to be loved by only ourselves.

But as I watched my daughters smile while their father fell apart in a hospital across town, I knew these were truths to be learned only through experience.

I could finally see it.

For two decades I had been tormented by the guilt of not being able to carry my mother's grief. I had run away from her over and over again, distancing myself from the weight of an impossible burden she never asked me to bear. Drowned by her unexpressed sadness, I had been trying to buoy her when all she needed was for someone to hold her while she sank.

To cradle her head and whisper "it's okay, it's okay, it's okay."

CHAPTER 8

Though it is impossible to carry pain for another, a mother's emotions are never separate from her child's. What beauty and what terror, to experience this kind of love—one that walks the line between growth and collapse. Once a child is placed in our tired arms, our hearts are forever tethered. To become a mother is to lose and find yourself, to build worlds inside you only to give them away.

I was once a sixteen-year-old living in a van with a twenty-two-year-old AWOL Mormon missionary; I was once an eighteen-year-old wayward Mormon dating a twenty-four-year-old meth addict in LA, all while my mother grieved the loss of her husband. Only now do I wonder how my decisions back then affected her. Did she measure herself by the fallout of my recklessness? Had my rage dictated her self-worth? Was her happiness compromised by my choices?

These questions demand an agonizing accountability because the answer to each is a resounding yes, yes, yes. While trying to carry my mother's sadness, I was also contributing to it.

* * *

I was accepted to Brigham Young University–Hawaii a few months after Dylan's relapse with Alberto. After a dizzying swing of drunken nights and brown buildings, we decided that change would bring us back together and help him stay sober.

Despite my adolescent delinquency, I managed to excel in school and was accepted to a few universities in Canada. Mum pushed for BYUH, a Mormon institution, with the hope that being surrounded by members of the church would rectify my unruly path and lead me back to happiness, and maybe even her.

In the end I chose BYUH because its campus was located on a tropical island and the only one Dylan could follow me to, since his prior felony drug charges barred him from international travel. But my admission was contingent upon two potential roadblocks: the Honor Code and the Ecclesiastical Endorsement.

The Honor Code was a contractual agreement to abstain from drugs, coffee, alcohol, and premarital sex both on and off campus for the duration of my studies—in other words, to uphold the standards outlined in Mormonism's Word of Wisdom commandment given as revelation from god to its founder Joseph Smith in 1833. The Honor Code creed was outlined by the "Student Word of Honor," a quote written on the official form by revered LDS educator Karl G. Maeser:

> Place me behind prison walls—walls of stone ever so high, ever so thick, reaching ever so far in the ground—there is a possibility that in some way or another I may be able to escape. But stand me on that floor and draw a chalk line around me and have me give my word of honor never to cross it. Can I get out of that circle? No, never! I'd die first.

I signed the contract without hesitation, fully intent on crossing the chalk line given the first opportunity. I would just need to be mindful to not get caught, as the consequence of violating its strict enforcement was suspension or expulsion.

The Ecclesiastical Endorsement, on the other hand, would be more involved than a disingenuous signature. As an official approval letter declaring that I was "worthy" to attend the religious university, this endorsement would require a sit-down interview with my childhood bishop. I had a decent understanding of what "worthy" meant in my religion, and I knew I wouldn't pass the interview if I offered any semblance of truth.

"What do I tell him?" I asked Mum on the way to the bishop's interview, my question mitigated by the foregone pretense that I was an obedient daughter of god. I was in Montreal for the summer to prepare for Hawaii, and Mum had been helping me get things in order with a giddiness I hadn't seen in her in years.

Bishop Huang had been kind to me as a child, but the thought of confessing my transgressions to a man I barely knew felt unjust. I didn't have the language to express the oppression one feels as a child confessing her "sins" to a middle-aged man for divine exoneration or an approval of worthiness. At the time, it all just felt like *fuck the police*.

Mum's eyes were fixed ahead as we passed rows of manicured maple trees that lined the suburban roads leading to my church. Deep down I think she felt the dissonance—that there was something sickening about the confession-absolution dialectic of misogyny that existed in our religion. I want to believe that she did.

"Just tell him what feels right to say," she said.

We pulled into the parking lot, the emptiness of the church on a weekday evening only adding to my unease. The building looked strange without the mayhem of worship and churchgoers vying to reach the pews on time, without mothers fixing their daughters' hair in car mirrors or fathers straightening their ties before entering the house of god because god forbid they were late or sloppy. What would the other members think?

I shuddered as Mum idled at the entrance.

"You'll be fine, Steph," she said. She gave me a rallying pat on the leg, radiating with hope. It was a nice feeling—to feel that kind of promise directed at me.

I walked into the church to find Bishop Huang waiting for me in the front foyer, his kind smile a stark contrast against his tailored suit and tie. It was the same uniform Matt had worn when we met.

The bishop made small talk as he escorted me to his office, which, as I learned at a young age, was a place reserved for praise or punishment and all manner of black and white. We followed the hallways I had walked as a child, past the water fountain where Phil and I filled up the sacrament cups we stole when Mum wasn't looking, and around the Sunday school room where I had learned of faith and perfection. Finally, reverently and quietly, we crossed the back foyer where I had first met Matt and stopped in front of the bishop's office. Opening the door, Bishop Huang extended his arm and invited me into a room humbly decorated with stacks of books and a single framed painting of Jesus intervening in a stormy shipwreck, saving a crew of fishermen.

Selective miracles, I thought as I sat in the chair opposite his desk, trying to avoid Jesus's sympathetic eyes.

"It's good to see you, Sister Catudal. Now, tell me why you chose BYU–Hawaii," the bishop said, glancing down at his checklist.

"Does the applicant live a chaste and virtuous life, including the avoidance of pornography, abstinence from sexual relations outside of marriage, and abstinence from homosexuality?"

"Does the applicant live the Word of Wisdom by abstaining from alcoholic beverages, tobacco, coffee, tea, and drug abuse?"

Caged by shame and the desire to ease my mother's sadness, the truth groped at my throat: I wanted to live by the ocean and help pull my boyfriend away from the allure of crack cocaine. Instead, I rattled off platitudes about being surrounded by good influences in a positive environment.

"That's nice, Stephanie. Now—is there something that weighs on you? Is there anything that makes you feel like you might hinder your worthiness to attend an LDS institution?"

I looked up, glancing towards Jesus at sea. Was it really sympathy in his eyes? If he *was* real, what kind of god would shame an eighteen-year-old girl for her pain?

Fuck it, I thought and divulged my transgressions—covering every topic of sin other than murder, including the handful of morning-after pills I'd taken over the years. I wasn't sure why I chose to be truthful when I could have easily lied. Perhaps it was an archaic sense of religious guilt that had been ingrained in me at a young age. Maybe I was intimidated by the idea of attending a Mormon school and wanted to sabotage my chances of admittance. More than anything, it was cathartic to list all the ways I'd defied god for saving those fishermen and not my father.

"So, yeah . . . I understand if you can't sign it," I said once I'd finished, pointing to the endorsement paper Mum had printed off earlier that day before handing it to me like a gold medal, shining with promise.

Bishop Huang lowered his head. Was it prayer or shame? The two always seemed to be intertwined.

"Let me ask you again, Sister Catudal. Why do you want to attend an LDS institution?"

I paused. Was there a more worthy answer?

"I want to be better," I blurted, surprising even myself, and for once it felt honest. It was almost an admission, though I didn't really know what it meant. I wasn't sure whether *better* would rein me into Jesus's embrace like my religion suggested, or if it was something that instead lived inside me. Was *better* a pair of divine footsteps extending across a stormy sea? Or was it something I had to dig to find inside myself?

Nodding his head, Bishop Huang signs my endorsement, checking the "without reservation" box, because someone in a suit and tie once decided that my worthiness was a sliding scale. That my worth was determined by a three-tiered checklist:

Worthy, without reservation.

Worthy, with reservation.

Unworthy.

Then he shakes my hand and stares into my eyes until I look away, down at my Converse that I've covered in inverted crosses and anarchy symbols. I walk back to the car feeling cheated by his kindness, the same way I felt betrayed by the benevolent cop who'd ended my runaway three years earlier. I sit in my mum's car, writhing in the discomfort of another broken stereotype as I replay his last words in my mind.

"I'm going to tell you the truth, Sister Catudal. None of those things really matter. I see your heart. And it is good."

* * *

It was mid-August when I landed alone in Honolulu with my skateboard, a carry-on suitcase, and a printed receipt for a shuttle to BYU–Hawaii, located an hour up the northeast side of Oahu.

The salty air was palpable, the humidity stifling as I walked off the airplane and onto the island that would become my new home. I followed the flow of passengers through sliding glass doors and out into the night air that smelled of plumerias and brine. I breathed it in with pursed lips, eager to taste it all.

I had decided to leave for Oahu a week before the new student arrival date, anxious to get acquainted with the island without the pressure of socializing. In my mind, every Mormon at the university would see my tattoos and embark on a crusade to save my soul. For the time being, I didn't know a single person in Hawaii, and I wanted to keep it that way for as long as possible.

The university grounds were silent when the shuttle dropped me off long after campus curfew. I pulled my suitcase down the pristine sidewalk—an echoing reminder that I was a disturbance of reverence. I walked down the dimly lit pathway flanked by international flags and palm trees, smiling as a warm breeze rippled through my sweat-soaked clothes. Even as an outsider in this place, Hawaii felt like another new beginning. Anyways, I had grown quite comfortable being a disturbance.

I wandered around campus for a while before finding my assigned dorm building and its designated RA, who was deep in a world of late-night board games with her friends. After exchanging pleasantries and declining to join the winning Pictionary team, I was escorted to where I would sleep for the next seven days. Since I had arrived early, my dorm room wasn't ready. For now, the only accommodation they could offer was the floor of the piano room.

Resting my skateboard against the wall, I thanked the RA before making a bed next to one of the room's upright pianos with the sheet and pillow she had handed me. I was happy to have the room to myself, especially in such close proximity to this hallowed musical instrument. As I nestled under the piano's sturdy frame, I was reminded of my paternal grandpapa, who died when I was ten years old.

"Un, deux, trois, quatre, la da da da," I can hear him whisper as he sways to the count of my off-beat rhythm, his finger ticking like a metronome. I am five when he starts teaching me how to play on his 1901 baby grand Steinway concert piano. A musically inclined man with a propensity for alcoholism and depression, Grandpapa was a renowned jazz pianist in Montreal in the sixties and seventies. Over the years, both age and lithium softened his ability to play the piano, but never his love for it. Instead, he channels that love into teaching me—the only one of us four siblings who feels a deep connection to the flow of arpeggios and scales.

"Trop vite, Stephie. Too fast, there is no rush." Pointing to the sheet music he's written by hand, Grandpapa asks that I start the prelude once more as Dad looks on from the kitchen and smiles, the smell of decaf coffee permeating the evening air.

I spend hours sitting on that cushioned bench, my fingers flowing over the ivory keys while Dad listens from his La-Z-Boy. His eyes are closed, and a smile is stretched across his face. As I grow older, I wonder if Grandpapa felt this way when he danced through the octaves—weightless, apart, at peace.

When Dad gets sick three years after Grandpapa dies, he tells me that my music is one of the only things that lessens his pain. And I guess in some way it lessens mine too, if only for the moment. The piano is my first encounter with holy gateways and conduits of escape—my first experience with being between time and space.

On the night of Dad's death, Phil and I sit on the floor next to the piano playing Mad Libs, giggling as we read "The dog likes to carry buttholes in its mouth." I make sure to laugh hard so Phil won't feel shame in the everythingness of laughter when our dad's body lies dead a few doors down.

And the piano stands open to death and laughter, accepting of all the sadness that has been poured into her over the years. Fluid despite the suffering she has grounded. Worthy of harmony despite all the pain.

The night he died, I vowed to be more like her, stoic yet open somehow. Still, I couldn't bring myself to sit at her bench anymore. I couldn't bear to play an instrument that held the melodies of my memories tragic and sweet, though I wasn't sure there was a difference anymore—between love and pain. They, too, always seemed to be wrapped around each other.

In this intersection, curled next to the cold metal pedals in an otherwise empty room in Hawaii, I felt at home for the first time in a long time.

Maybe tomorrow I'd sit on the bench and see if my fingers remembered the weight of the keys.

Or perhaps, more importantly, if they could forget the weight of them.

But memory is eternal. It is alive.

There are certain events that will live forever, particular sounds that will never leave me, feelings I will never forget. They stick to my bones, coming back in flashes like a fever dream in the dead of night.

I used to curse my memory. Now I wonder if it is a vehicle for the lessons that fold in on themselves, reminders of what I didn't hear the first time around.

CHAPTER 9

Two weeks after Rivs's admission to the ICU my phone was a siren in the night. It was long after midnight and the stagnant heat of mid-July hung heavily in our bedroom. Suffocating, almost, without the usual hiss of wild winds blustering through our home. The night was strangely quiet, or perhaps that's just how I remember it—a sharp contrast splitting my world in two.

I shot out of bed like a sentinel sleeping on duty, fumbling in the dark to answer the call, though I'd been preparing myself for it all along, though I'd spent the past twenty years on watch for the downturn between love and tragedy.

"Hello, Stephanie?"

The voice was calm but urgent, calculated but rushed.

"Yes?"

I sat on the edge of my bed and planted my feet on the floor in a feigned declaration of strength. I understood the significance of a phone call rupturing the stillness of night. I was searching for firm ground when I knew the following words would leave me unmoored.

"Stephanie, this is Dr. Hemmerman. I'm the critical care doctor tonight. I'm here with your husband. His lungs are deteriorating quickly. He has displayed an incredible ability to function with low oxygen levels, but we can't wait any longer. We need to put him on a ventilator right now."

The world paused.

Only hours ago we'd been joking about biopsies and the bubonic plague. How quickly life can change with a single sentence. How swiftly we clamor for normal when tragedy gropes at our ordinary with greedy hands.

"Yes, okay. I understand," I said, clearing sleep from my throat. "Can you offer your theory on the origins of his lesions? Will he be stable during tomorrow's open lung biopsy? How long do you foresee his intubation?"

That morning, the results of his fine-needle biopsy had come back inconclusive. Hoping to yield a concrete diagnosis, the pulmonologist had ordered a more aggressive biopsy to be sent to the Mayo Clinic for pathology, which would require general anesthesia and a larger cross section of lung tissue.

"We don't have any answers yet. I'm sorry. We still can't figure out what is causing his lung failure. In his condition, just getting him stabilized on the ventilator tonight will be a challenge. We're going to have to fully sedate him for the duration of his intubation. Let's get him through that first."

"Yes, okay, thank you."

I hung up the phone and stared at the wall, my toes curled into the floor, searching for gravity. You could spend your whole life waiting and never be prepared for the airlessness of tragedy.

"It's too much," was all I could think. *"I can't do it. It's too much."*

Rivs called seconds later.

"It's going to be okay, babe," he said above the mechanical beeps and hushed commotion as the critical care team gathered in his room. "Don't worry, Steph. It's gonna be okay. I always come back. Remember?"

Him, comforting me from across town but a million miles away while doctors layered his body in blue surgical sheets. Him, video calling while being prepped for life support. I saw his lips move as he held the phone close to his mouth. I heard the doctors whisper "you need to say goodbye now," their urgency punctuating the severity of his circumstance.

"I gotta go. I'll probably be under for a few days. I sent messages to each of the girls. Please have them listen. Tell them not to worry. It's going to be okay. I promise."

The girls the girls the girls.

The breadth of my heart and an echo of phantom words I hadn't reconciled from my childhood.

Tell them not to worry.

A father's wish imbalanced against the weight of impossibility. I had been destroyed by the unabridged space between faith and reality. I had been a girl standing on the edge of hope and it swallowed me whole. The chasm was unending. It was a panic that no amount of bravery could tear through. There was no way to fall and come out unscathed.

How do you hold the grief of three children when you've barely discovered how to carry your own?

"Wait—are you scared?" I sobbed because tact is hopeless when death stares you down with familiar eyes.

"No, I'm not scared," he said, his voice unwavering. "Don't be scared, okay?"

"Okay."

"I'm gonna be okay. I promise. I love you, Steph."

And then the line was still. It was a deafening silence that cut through the night louder than any call. What a lonely thing, the lack of sound. I had never realized it before. Its ring was terrifying.

Can you scream "don't go" when you know spoken words hold little pull in the flume between life and death?

And still I tried.

"Rivs? Rivs!"

The bedroom collapsed with quiet. I dropped the phone and ran for my mum who was asleep in our basement. She had flown in earlier that morning to help me care for our girls once Tawny had left, now that my days were filled with medical research and hospital runs to drop off Rivs's bedside requests that dwindled as the days dragged on: Nutter

Butters, ear plugs, Chipotle burritos hidden under pairs of sweatpants and dropped off at the COVID-19 reception area for mournful families.

The basement was lifetimes away as my mind was overwhelmed by memories of the covetousness of disease and lives cut short. I thought about my dad and how he hadn't been scared at the end of his life. I thought about my mum, who was seemingly unmoved in the face of death. I thought about how I was turning out to be far less like my parents than I once imagined. Mostly, I thought of my sweet girls and the firsthand knowledge that time does not heal all wounds.

I resented knowing these things so intimately.

The girls the girls the girls.

How would I tell them? What would I say? Up until that point my children understood that their dad's lungs were sick. They knew that the doctors were trying everything to help him get better, but that it would be a long recovery. They seemed to accept this glossy explanation and didn't ask many questions. They were comforted by FaceTime calls to the hospital, when Rivs had been sure to stifle his cough and hold his phone close to avoid showing the tubes and machines. My daughters believed their father was immortal just like I had believed mine to be, and I didn't correct them. Even knowing all that I did about hope and reality, I left them as children tucked high between the branches while the ground crumbled beneath them.

I let them believe.

Mum shot up in bed when I cracked the basement door, forever a sentinel herself. Following her example, I tried to be strong as I walked through the door, but a sob escaped my lips as I walked towards her.

"Oh, Steph," she said.

I sat on the bed beside her. She switched on the light and here we were together, two wives of breathless husbands.

She held my gaze. I wasn't sure if it was sympathy or responsibility in her eyes. Likely it was both—extremes meeting on the precipice of a knowing stare.

"They're sedating him. They're putting him on a ventilator right now, Mum," I cried, leaning closer into her.

"Oh, Steph, oh, Steph." She pulled me in and wrapped an arm around my shoulder.

Tonight my husband was suffocating the same way hers had been at the end of his life, when he had pulled for air in our computer room.

"Do you want me to sleep in your bed tonight?"

I nodded, caught between innocence and knowing, feeling like my mother's child for the first time in a long time.

My mum. She knew. My god she knew better than anyone.

And there it was, splayed out for me like Christmas dinner, one of the many epiphanies that would come to me like gatherings around a table reserved only for special occasions, a meeting of generational wisdom that would unfurl in blooms of perennial knowing like gifts borne of pain.

When my father died, I only thought about what I had lost. I never considered that my mother's husband had died that night, too. It was a truth I hadn't communed with.

She knows what it feels like.

She knows how I feel.

She feels.

What a blessing and a curse, to learn in an instant that pain is the intercessor of empathy.

For the first time in a long time, all I wanted was my mother.

It's okay, it's okay, it's okay.

* * *

During the first few days of Rivs's induced coma, I tried to be strong for my girls. I forced myself to smile for them, to feed them healthy meals and engage in normal activities. I tried to do what Mum had done for us when Dad was sick—offer some semblance of normalcy in a deeply abnormal time. But as the days unfolded, I started to realize that an effigy of strength might not be what my daughters needed most. Instead, I revealed the humanness of my sorrow.

I began to unravel before them, exposing my sadness and fear.

And they held space for it all in their astonishing ability to view life with kaleidoscopic range. Rather than place value or judgment on emotion, children allow themselves to experience multiple feelings at once. For children, everything just *is*.

So we laughed and we cried together. We told silly jokes and yelled angrily at each other in misplaced rage. Some nights we ate chicken and broccoli, other nights we ordered McDonald's and ate ice cream straight from the tub. We took long walks in the woods and lay around in bed watching movies.

All the while I allowed myself to feel rising waves of sadness and fear within a pooling tide of gratitude and love. It was something I had never done as a child, feel the swing of mortality without the promise of an everlasting tomorrow. It was life in all of its opposition, sharp and gray all at once.

I didn't know if it was damaging or freeing for my children to see me experience the fullness of human emotion, but it was all I could do.

Allow.

Because I had never allowed myself to feel it all. As I moved through my childhood grief, the immensity of its wholeness was far too big to take in at once.

Truth, memory, emotion; the things that may fester inside can also drown us if we set them free before we're ready.

My grief had always been a slow drain. There was no finality to it. All I could do was take tiny sips, drink from the well in rations small enough to keep myself from sinking.

CHAPTER 10

It was in early September, three weeks after my arrival to Hawaii, that I drove to Honolulu in my roommate's beat up Honda Civic to get Dylan from the airport. The air was wet and warm on my hand extended out the car's open window as lines of palm trees blurred by, swaying in the soggy evening breeze. As with most Hawaiian beater cars, the air conditioner had stopped working long before my roommate handed someone five hundred dollars on the side of the road in exchange for a set of keys.

I breathed in deep and released a spirited whoop into the quiet night. I was free, living on my own for the first time, far from friends or family or anyone who knew me, far from pitying looks that said, "you poor girl, look what life and death have done to you," far from people who weighed the old me against the new and decided that grief is a cunning beast, greedy and grave.

Like LA, Hawaii was another opportunity to reinvent myself, only this time I had no older sister to disappoint, no mother checking in to keep tabs. The only thought that blunted my sense of freedom was Dylan, who was flying to the island later that evening.

I drove down the dark country highway towards the lights of Waikiki with a looming sense that I was winding my way towards someone I had outgrown.

I broke up with him twelve days later.

"But I love you so much," Dylan tendered, as though words were a currency that could pay the toll for the space between us. He looked crushed, like when we walked arm in arm towards the little brown buildings in LA.

He sobbed into my chest and I held him close. I was scared to let him go—a vestige of my former self.

"I love you too," I whispered, aching for familiarity in a foreign place though the syllables felt unnatural on my tongue now that I was committed to my new beginning, desperate for the *better* I had suggested to Bishop Huang.

Dylan hung around the island for a few weeks after our breakup, living in a car he bought using the last of his final paycheck from Starbucks. I'd see him around town quite often, sitting alone on the beach or skateboarding down the sidewalks near campus. Usually we'd hug and exchange pleasantries before I'd have to run to class or off to surf with new friends, and each time I was certain that I'd made the right choice.

As much as I had distanced myself from religious dogma, the idea that action was the principal measure of morality was a deeply ingrained concept. I was revolted by the hypocrisy of Christian judgment, but the notion was buried inside me, posited like a weapon against my self-worth. I had never considered the truth of Bishop Huang's words, that betterness might be more accurately gauged by things outside of checklists and laws.

But after several weeks playing the role of model BYU student, I grew tired of the stillness. Entrenched in the epicenter of Mormon culture, I was reminded why I resented my religion, from the platitudes on faith and miracles to the notion that obedience would lead to blessings and happiness. I was frustrated by campus modesty rules that seemed to only apply to women—ones that wouldn't allow me to show my knees or shoulders, even in the stifling Hawaiian heat. I was enraged by the church's antiquated views on gay marriage and the gender roles that permeated every aspect of student life. Most of all, as I started to learn about Hawaiian history and the unfolding of its recent colonization, I was angered by the idea that this white-owned institution had purchased swaths of sacred land and evicted Indigenous inhabitants from their birthright in order to expand "The Lord's Kingdom on Earth."

The allure of my Hawaii dream dissolved with the realization that I was just another white settler carrying out a soft crusade.

But the spirit of rebellion is kinetic, and it wasn't long before I found BYUH's small population of Mormon dissidents.

First, I met Marina, a Brazilian student with caramel skin and smoldering brown eyes. Gliding past me on a skateboard down the circular campus roads, I remember thinking that she was the most beautiful woman I had ever seen. Raised in the União do Vegetal, an Amazonian religion that revered the psychedelic ayahuasca as a divine sacrament, Marina found the rigidity of Mormonism laughable. Still, she didn't hesitate when presented with the opportunity to attend BYUH under its international student scholarship program, which aimed to diversify its student body. Throughout her life, Hawaii had been one of Marina's top bucket-list destinations. Being surrounded by a bunch of Mormons seemed like a small price to pay to be able to live here.

After finishing our first semester in the dorms, Marina and I moved into a small house a few hundred yards away from the beach, less than a mile from campus. We surfed, skated, and drank our way through the next semester, sneaking boys and handles of liquor past our Mormon roommates.

For a while we believed we were the only two renegades on campus, but we soon discovered a small network of partying Mormons. It was like striking water after weeks of digging, the flood of rebellious commiseration quenching our oppressed thirst.

We played the Mormon game well, following dress standards and attending weekly church activities with postured devotion while discussing clandestine party plans in the university's outdoor hallways. We were furtive in our ways, since being accused of drinking alcohol warranted a trip to the Honor Code office for questioning and, if found guilty, expulsion.

Knowing our chances of getting caught decreased the further we were from campus, each weekend the group of six or seven of us would load into Marina's car, sitting on laps or curled on floor mats to make the hour-long drive to Waikiki. Sometimes her car would start on the first try and we would cheer with excitement. Other times one of us would have to squeeze out of the overloaded vehicle to hit the starter with a can opener—which I soon learned was a car owner's rite of passage on the island. On days when the car wouldn't start, we nixed our Waikiki plans and elected someone to hitch a ride to the next town over to buy a few bottles of cheap rum.

As with many things in life, one thing led to another. Like Dylan and the Coronas, my grief required elevated mitigations to be kept at bay. Once the subduing effects of alcohol had been reached, I moved on.

My love affair with MDMA began the night we met Steve at an after-hours club on a Saturday night in Waikiki. He was heavyset and sloppily dressed, sitting on a black couch that lined Galaxy Nightclub's dance floor, one of the newer clubs in our weekly rotation. In understated coolness that denoted importance, he appeared unamused by the swaths of people swarming around him.

"I bet he's a drug dealer!" Marina yelled above the deafening techno music booming through the grimy club.

I shrugged my shoulders and agreed. Despite my relationship with Dylan, I still had little experience with drug dealers.

Making her way through the crowd, Marina walked towards the couch and leaned over Steve. His face lit up when he looked to see a towering beauty in frayed jean shorts standing in front of him.

"Hey, gorgeous," he said, taking her hand and motioning for her to sit. Marina sat close to him on the couch and whispered in his ear. Then he nodded before leading her towards the bathroom.

She returned moments later with Steve by her side and a sly grin on her face.

"This shit will make your clit tingle," Steve whispered, pulling me close with one hand and placing a small blue pill in the other.

I was reminded of my singular experience with weed and haunted by the torment I'd seen Dylan endure. For as reckless as I wanted to be, drugs scared me.

"What is it?" I asked.

"Ecstasy," he replied.

I looked around the room and watched as each one of my new friends swallowed Steve's offering without a second thought.

"Fuck it," I said, which seemed to be the new theme of my life. I popped the pill in my mouth.

When it kicks in, I feel a wave of gentle intensity growing up my spine. It pulses through my veins, shimmering from the tips of my toes and out through my limbs like a familiar embrace.

I've never felt more loved or less afraid in my life. In the euphoric haze of release my anger fades away. With each inhale my sadness bubbles and recedes, cradled by love in the womb of acceptance. Everything is both heightened and softened. All of the pain, all of the darkness I've ever experienced is held without judgment.

I am flowing over the keys of time and space. I am gliding through empathy with my eyes closed, my head tilted back in bliss, both universally aware and oblivious at the same time. Everything that was ever mundane is now sacred—a touch, a breath, a stare, a Skittle.

Tonight, I am a child again. Everything just is.

When I finally opened my eyes, I noticed Steve gravitating towards Marina.

I touched her arm to make sure she was comfortable with his closeness. Her skin was velvet on my fingers. We were intrinsically connected, our souls fused by a single touch. With an angelic smile she lifted her chin and whispered the truest phrase I'd ever heard.

"This feels like home."

And for a while, ecstasy was our home.

We grew close to Steve, who supplied us with free pills in exchange for friendship. Ecstasy became an obsession—a sacrament I partook multiple times a week, desperate for the forgiveness it gave so will-

ingly without the intermediary of a bishop, or any man for that matter.
Eventually it required five pills to sustain the high I'd felt on that first
night—my redemption found only in extremes.

It wasn't happiness I felt during that time, but it felt like something
close. After years of sipping my grief, acceptance was a drink of freedom. In my limited view of the term, happiness was a fleeting glimmer
up my spine and peace was nothing more than the ability to feel nothing
at all.

One year later, Marina was called to BYUH's Honor Code office,
where she was met by two coast guard officers. Standing in full uniform
they explained that Marina and I were the primary contacts found in
Petty Officer Steven Malrouney's phone, who had been court martialed
on charges of drug trafficking. Marina bravely denied knowing Steve
but called me in a panic as soon as she left the Honor Code office that
afternoon.

"Holy shit I just lied to the coast guard! *And* the Honor Code office.
How did they find us?"

"I don't know, but they left a voicemail on my phone while I was in
class!"

Later that night we leafed through the Oahu yellow pages for "At-
torney" and landed on the most obnoxious advertisement we could
find.

"Day or Night, Atn. Monty Allen is By Your Side" the ad said, the
tacky script overlaid on top of a picture of a man in a smart cobalt suit.
Feeling satisfied with our choice, we bookmarked the page.

At eight the next morning, with our ears competing over a landline,
Marina and I explained our situation to Monty, oscillating between
nervous stutters and stifled giggles. Monty listened intently before
giving us invaluable information: civilians were rarely subpoenaed for
court martial trials. Upon hearing this news, we thanked him and
ended the call. Falling back on Marina's bed, we rolled with laughter
and congratulated each other for our loyalty and courage.

But as the weeks passed, the novelty of our encounter with the law wore off and we mourned the loss of our drug hookup. I wondered what life would look like without the steady flow of ecstasy and its emancipating effects. Other than a single prison call made to Marina, we never heard from Steve again, and after weeks of missed calls and ignored voicemails, the coast guard stopped calling.

Over a shared bottle of rum and rounds of snorted Adderall, Marina and I belly laughed until our sides hurt that Monty Allen had been right after all.

I finished the semester feeling low and anxious despite the turquoise waters and trade wind warmth of Hawaiian spring. In the midst of serotonin withdrawal, compounded by a phone call I received from Dylan telling me that Alberto had passed away, paradise had lost its allure.

The anger I had been avoiding returned with a vengeance. I was restless in my skin, itching to leave the island but not wanting to go home to Montreal for summer break. I wanted to honor the exemplary gratitude Alberto had taught, but all I felt was rage.

When one of my professors mentioned a volunteer group traveling to Guatemala for the summer, I believed it was the answer I had been looking for. Because I also believed that betterness was something to be reached, something to be traveled to, something to be atoned for.

I was a child of kindling grief just trying to keep my head above the smoke.

CHAPTER 11

Four days had passed since the night Rivs was sedated and put on a ventilator. The hours dragged on as my daughters' grief compounded with my own. Even knowing what I did about sorrow and its unshareable burden, I still tried to tear through the thick of it, desperate to carry it all. How could I not?

Bearing the weight of a child's sorrow is impossible, and as a mother you still try. Even when it's futile, even when you know you can't save them. Even when it means drowning yourself—you still try. We give it all to them though we know they'll hurt the same without our sacrifice.

And I would choose to carry it over and over again for the faint chance that it might, in some way, ease my children's pain.

Now I wonder if perhaps it wasn't sympathy I'd seen in Jesus's eyes all those years ago, in that painting in Bishop Huang's office. Perhaps there had been no altruism in divine deliverance, no redemption in the squall. Maybe for Jesus, becoming a savior was just plain responsibility. Maybe he had rescued those fishermen because what other choice do you have when shouldering the future? What else can you do when salvation depends on the unanswerable question you still find yourself asking:

My god, my god, why hast thou forsaken me?

As Rivs wrestled life and death, I tried to stabilize myself on faltering ground. I tried to escort my girls to the imagined banks of safety with the same insolvable question.

Weren't you just right here?

I had been in this space before, with my dad after he went into a coma on my birthday. Back then, I was certain he was gone. I had no hope that his soul was free and in some better place, or that he was closer to me than ever before, as my religion suggested. My disappointment with miracles led me to be convinced of the finite nature of existence. While my dad slept on the edges of mortality, I accepted that his light was quickly fading.

I remember feeling his intangibility when I walked into his room. It felt empty, as if he was already gone. Him, the immovable man. And there we were the rest of us, silently begging to let him live, to let him die, to *please dear Lord, anything but this.*

(My god, my god.)

Mum is in the kitchen cooking dinner and humming a church hymn, reverent and faithful.

I am doing homework next to Phil on the dining room table. Rachel is with Dad, reading him articles from an outdated National Geographic. *Dave is out with friends, anywhere but here.*

Even with death hanging heavy, a pencil scratches out ninth-grade algebra, lips read from an old magazine, a preheated oven beeps, Dad takes his last breaths.

My god, my god.

Sometimes, the in-between is worse than death.

Since then, I had grown comfortable with the idea that existence was temporary—that death was a decisive return to the earth. I was satisfied with being a biological specimen devoid of everlasting potential and with life having no inherent meaning.

My experience with psychedelics had cracked the door on the possibility of eternity, or at least the notion of some everlasting connective force, though the feeling hadn't trickled down into my daily cosmology. The notion of an afterlife still seemed like a placation—a fairy tale to soften the finality of death.

With Rivs, everything felt different. It was a rolling surge in my soul, delicate and slowly rising. When I closed my eyes at night, I could almost find him—not with words but in *feeling*. In the quietude of his sedation, I felt a sense that Rivs was *somewhere*. I just didn't know where.

* * *

The hours dragged on in silence from his side of the universe, other than my nightly calls to nurses who whispered crippling words like "critical" and "we don't know what else we can do for him" in apologetic tones.

Doctors were baffled by his illness, which continued to deteriorate despite rounds of high dose steroids and antibiotics. While awaiting pathology results from his open lung biopsy, I learned from his nurses that Rivs's doctors had all but given up on his case. They agreed that his incredible fitness gave him an advantage in the fight against this unknown lung illness, but without a diagnosis there was little more that could be done. In spite of their best efforts, the lesions were continuing to grow at an alarming rate. His pulmonary X-ray was now a clouded mass of white. There was hardly any functional space remaining in his lungs.

"Don't you know he's my husband?" I would have wanted to yell if I ever had the chance to speak with a doctor. "Can't you see he's their father? Don't you know what happens to little girls when dads die?"

Words that had been screamed hundreds of thousands of times as the COVID-19 death toll continued to climb were now fighting to escape my lips. I thought them with vehemence, though I knew mine were no more important than the same words screamed by other husbands, wives, fathers, daughters, mothers, and sons. These faceless statistics were *people*—not numbers on a television screen but human beings with entire lives in front of them, or behind them, or depending on them.

"You need to advocate for him," his nurse, Tara, pleaded on one of my evening calls. "*You're* his voice now. You need to call the doctors and demand answers. You can't let them give up on him. He's not done. Don't let him be done."

I was grateful for the nursing staff's dedication to Rivs when it felt like his physicians had moved on, but the idea that I had to step into a role of power when I was falling apart felt like too much.

This was the thought that cut through the fog: my husband might die in silence because I couldn't find the courage to speak up.

I was born into a world that was diametrically opposed to the discovery of my inherent power. Like most girls of my generation, I was taught that strength was an extraneous force—a nebula to be chased through the heavens. The myth of my innocence had faded long ago, but in some ways I was still a little girl waiting to be rescued. A prince, a god, a Savior, a lover, a pill—while the fables changed, my belief in them remained.

* * *

The next morning, Tara introduced me to the term "end of life."

"We're not classifying him as 'end of life' yet, but if or when we do, you'll be able to come in and see him. He's been very difficult to sedate. Every time we move him his oxygen drops. He just can't seem to calm down. He keeps fighting the ventilator. Maybe having you here will help him. We're really sorry you can't come in yet. We're all advocating for you to be here."

Perhaps it was self-preservation that led me to deny how close he was to death. Maybe I'd convinced myself that Rivs *was* immortal—some mythological creature gifted to me as penance for a dead father. No matter what, he always came back.

That day the fantasy faded, mired between the torment of two adverbs, the heaviness of those syllables an anvil on my chest.

When.

Yet.

I'd never known words to hold such crushing mass.

For the first time I was beginning to think that Rivs might not make it. The privileged but comforting lie I'd told myself—that tragedy has a lifetime quota—dissolved around me.

That same afternoon, Julie flew in from Oregon, once Rivs could no longer placate his mother with assurances of his health. During that time and throughout his illness, she and my mother absorbed all the things I could not, from managing a household to shouldering my daughters' emotions. They led me through the bleakest days when I was flailing in the obscurity of sadness and fear. Though they could never take away my pain, they lessened its burden by holding me in the intersessional power that is borne of love. (*It's okay, it's okay, it's okay.*)

Now that I have the prescience to step back and understand all they did for me, I am in awe. I had never before understood the immensity of their strength, because it was a steel that mothers rarely acknowledge. They were simply doing what women have always done: hold worlds together in shadowed recognition.

It was a tale as old as time, both commonplace and extraordinary: when I couldn't do it alone, I was carried forward by women bearing all that I could not.

* * *

The morning before his intubation and sedation, Rivs had made a series of Instagram videos attempting to explain, through the fog of narcotic delirium, the reason for his hospitalization. He laughed as he mentioned the plague, then explained his low platelet count and the hypothesis that he was suffering from a new and undecipherable strain of COVID-19. In disjointed sentences he described some of the procedures he'd had, from the fine-needle lung biopsy to the subsequent collapsed lung and painful chest tube. But mostly, he chose to speak of the power of love, the fragility of life, and the importance of being kind.

And all the while, in shortened sentences punctuated by gasping breaths behind a BiPAP mask, the numbers on his oxygen monitor changed from green to red, dropping from 88, to 83, to 79 and below.

Beeps and alarms. The ear-splitting hiss of oxygen. The calm on Rivs's face as nurses shuffled into his room, when he flashed a guilty grin to his phone camera, the kindness in his eyes still visible despite his swollen eyelids. All of this is seared in my mind as the last time I saw Rivs awake and alert, even if only through a cell phone screen.

Distance is relative when you are far away but still right here, feeling it all.

Despite his composure and assurances that he'd pull through like he always did, everyone watching Rivs's videos could see that he was struggling. From retracting ribs that pulled in with each inhale to nostrils flaring for every bit of hard-earned air, it was clear that he was in bad shape.

After that day, our family was the recipient of incredible love and support from within the Flagstaff community and around the world. It was staggering—a real-time example of the collective power of love binding humanity through pain. During that time, I felt more love than I'd ever experienced in my life. It was palpable; a tangible current of energy was holding our grieving family. It was carrying us through.

Still I felt so lonely, lonely despite the love that surrounded me. My mother. Julie. Rivs's family. My girls. My sister who would be at my side if only I asked. My two brothers tirelessly researching alternative lung injury treatments. Friends that had set up a meal service for our family. The outpouring of messages and support from around the world.

I had more love than one could hope for, and still I felt so lonely. It had always been in this space, in the disparity between my mind and my heart, that I felt the depths of my loneliness. I flayed in the blinding awareness that what I *should* be feeling wasn't what I *actually* felt. Surrounded by love yet feeling so alone—that is loneliness.

It is an isolation born of the inability to find mooring within. It is a bucket without a lid, a desperate gathering of love with nowhere to store it.

It all just floats away.

*　　*　　*

I am lying in bed adrift in inadequacy and untethered love. I feel unable to lead my daughters through tragedy. I am terrified that trauma will drag me back into the anger of my adolescence. I wonder how I'll make it through the uncertainty of each day. These fears circle above me in a darkness so real I feel it might consume me.

I lay in a bed that now feels cold and empty without Rivs asleep beside me, alone with the tragic realization I hope to carry with me for the rest of my life: it's the little things we miss. I watch in a vapid stare as the ceiling fan spins violently above me. I wonder if, like me, it is trying to balance a world on the verge of implosion.

Everything is caving in.

Once again I am inert—a fourteen-year-old daughter with a dead father, a thirty-four-year-old mother with a dying husband—both of us collapsing in grief.

I sink deep under my covers but nothing can warm me. The illusion that pain might be blanketed by love is long gone.

I feel so terribly lonely. So desperately afraid. So impossibly sad.

And then, in this desperate moment, I am shaken from my listless panic.

I hear the voice once again.

A booming knowing.

Another undeniable expression of wisdom.

A memory.

"This is not how he dies."

It is a stern shake and a warm embrace, a truth in every sense of the word.

A voice that speaks to the very code of my DNA, stirring memories of truth eternal. Something I've always known to be true.

It is more a command than a statement. It begs for action.

In the arid night of my fear I awake, wide eyed and resolute. And with palms wide open I stand in the power that has been growing inside me over the years, piece by piece. In the soils of tragedy I plant my feet in a strength that has been building all along. For the first time, I am grounded in myself. For the first time, I am home.

I sit up in bed, understanding the battle cry.

I hear you.

This is not how he dies.

I hear you.

CHAPTER 12

I left for Guatemala at the end of the spring semester, a few months before my twentieth birthday. Before being accepted to the program, I committed myself to a new Honor Code contract, pledging abstinence from alcohol, drugs, and sex for the duration of my stay with the Mormon-run NGO. I had no intention of honoring the code but signed it regardless, reasoning that it would be near impossible to find Molly or sneak alcohol into a house full of Mormons in a foreign country. I left Hawaii prepared for four months of sobriety and the distant chance that I might find *better* on the other side of the world.

I was met at the Guatemala City airport by eight volunteers who had flown in together from Utah, the epicenter of the LDS church. Together the nine of us lived in Chimaltenango, a mid-sized town on the bustling Pan-American Highway that smelled of burning wood and diesel exhaust. Our house was a small two-story compound lined with barbed wire and shards of broken glass cemented into a makeshift fence, our neighbors only a dozen feet away on either side and connected by a single laundry line strung between the yards.

I fell in love with Guatemala. I was captivated by the country, from its humble culture and stunning landscapes to the people who seemed to understand the secret to life: if you have enough, you don't need much else. After basic human needs are met, excess doesn't bring more happiness. Sadly, protracted conflict and generations of political instability made it difficult for many Guatemalans to meet their basic needs.

And still, despite regional hardships, the cultural sentiment shared by many Guatemalans was one of cautious gratitude.

It was at the end of a two-week project in the small mountain town of Xetenox that my experience shifted. We were implementing a pipeline to bring potable water to the isolated Mayan village and had spent long days working alongside the community, digging trenches and carrying PVC pipes over miles of dirt road. On our last day in the village, I watched four Mayan women cook our farewell feast over a communal outdoor fire pit. Wearing leather sandals and colorful hand-loomed blouses, I saw them lean towards each other in laughter as they labored over a large pot of steaming stock. Men sat around a hillside fire heating perfectly charred tortillas on red-hot rocks while shoeless children ran around grinning ear to ear, holding our hands and touching our skin with laughter and curiosity. Small adobe huts punctuated the rolling hills that painted the bucolic view with green in every direction. I took it all in, paralyzed by self-awareness and reminded of Alberto.

Here was a sense of community, of belonging, of purpose. Who was *I* to say that my way of life was better? More fulfilling? What exactly was *I* doing there? I had more comfort and had likely experienced less loss than the people of Xetenox. Where was *my* gratitude? Where was my happiness?

I left Xetenox painfully aware of my white savior complex, only then understanding the meaning of the word "ethnocentric"—a term I had learned in my anthropology class earlier that year. I had been judging Guatemala's cultural worth and happiness according to the standards of my own worldview. I had projected my values on a people who existed within a completely different context than my own.

It was then, standing among the beautiful hills of the Mayan countryside, that I recognized the truth of my anthropology professor's words: sustainable change doesn't originate from an outside source. It comes from within.

I went back to Chimaltenango struggling to justify that my work in Guatemala was positive in any endurable sense. Was I here only to absolve my conscience? To pay penance for my sins? To be *better*?

Luckily, because our volunteer group wasn't rigidly structured, we were encouraged to seek out humanitarian projects on our own. One afternoon while walking the colonial streets of Antigua—an expat hippie town lined with artisan vendor stalls and vegan cafes—I saw a volunteer ad for a sea turtle sanctuary in the coastal town of Monterrico. I could no longer rationalize "saving" other humans, but I saw no ethical dilemma in rescuing marine life.

After persuading our group leader that helping injured sea turtles in a beach town three hours south of Chimaltenango was indeed a humanitarian mission, I was given approval to travel to Monterrico for a week, provided that I bring along a companion. My closest friend in the group was Jane, a sweet blond-haired blue-eyed girl from Bountiful, Utah. She didn't hesitate when I asked her to join me.

Jane had never traveled outside of the southwestern United States before she was sent to Guatemala by her parents after they caught her snorting heroin in her bedroom. She was six months sober when she joined the volunteer program—a fact that the other group members didn't know.

Drawn by the pull of unspoken awareness, Jane and I became fast friends. We even attended a few AA meetings together after seeing the telltale triangular sign outside a run-down electronics store close to our Chimaltenango house. Sitting in a room full of middle-aged men, Jane and I sipped strong black coffee out of glass mugs as people shared stories of struggle and acceptance in a language we barely spoke. And somehow, it all felt familiar. Though awkwardly out of place amid the crowd of Guatemalan working men, we were welcomed with open arms. As I was coming to find, the intersection of love and pain was seldom lost in translation.

In its confluence, I was always home.

I think Jane felt that way, too. When I asked her to join me at the turtle sanctuary, she was easy to persuade despite her apprehension for adventure or travel.

Taking charge of our itinerary, I hired a microbus to Monterrico rather than navigate the somewhat unreliable local transit system. But the three-hour trip from Chimaltenango ended up lasting eight hours after our bus got a flat tire in the middle of a deep jungle.

Screeching to a stop on the side of a desolate dirt road, our driver hopped out of his seat and removed the flat tire without saying a word. After holding his open palm towards us through the window as if to signify "five minutes," or maybe "wait," he stood with it on the road under the shade of a ceiba tree. I glanced at the other two microbus passengers—a father and what appeared to be his young son. The father seemed annoyed by the situation but was otherwise calm. Observing his cool demeanor, I relaxed.

After twenty minutes of waiting without a single passing vehicle, we finally heard the grinding gears of a diesel school bus coming up from over a hill. Prefaced by a plume of exhaust, the colorful bus lumbered up the roadway, headed in the opposite direction of Monterrico. Clutching the blown tire under his arm, our driver flagged the bus down before jumping on its rear, leaving us without explanation and only a brief wave as he disappeared into the distance.

I looked over at Jane. She was sinking down in her seat, refusing to look out her open window—refusing to acknowledge that we were abandoned on the side of a Central American road with no one in sight for miles. Once again, I glanced at the father, who extended me a thumbs-up in reassurance.

"He'll be back," I said to Jane, more or less confident that it was true. "Come on. Let's walk around a bit."

Jane looked at me apprehensively but eventually gave up the safety of her seat and followed me out of the bus. The father and son climbed out as well, opting to rest in the shade.

Jane and I wandered together under the roadside tree line, trying to avoid the searing midday sun. Looking for something to cool us, I picked up a fallen mango, perfectly ripe and oozing with sticky sweetness. Peeling back its skin with my fingers, I handed the fruit to Jane as a token of apology.

"Come on, take a bite!" I said, eager to turn our precarious situation into a memorable adventure, or maybe searching for absolution.

Jane took the mango from my hand while I looked for another good one. A few minutes later we were laying under the cover of awning branches, gorging ourselves on amber flesh and laughing about where life had taken us.

"We're going to be okay, Jane," I said, truly believing it.

Our driver returned two hours later clutching the patched tire like a trophy, accompanied by two police officers who insisted on escorting our minivan the rest of the way to Monterrico. Through my growing understanding of Spanish, based on the foundation of French I grew up speaking, I overheard our driver tell the father about a similar microbus that had been robbed at gunpoint earlier that morning, less than two kilometers from where we had broken down.

It was late in the afternoon when Jane and I were dropped off in Monterrico's central plaza, along with the boy and his father. I wanted to thank them for unknowingly calming my nerves but didn't know how to say it in Spanish. Fumbling through my backpack, I handed the father a roadside mango and gave his son a high five. The father looked at the mango and smiled, perhaps seeing right through my saccharine offering of penitence.

"Wanna get some food before we go to the turtle place?" I asked Jane as we stepped off the bus, breathing in deep. The air held the same salinity as Hawaii. Purifying, almost.

She smiled and nodded, perhaps enjoying herself just a little. At least I told myself she was.

In broken Spanish I asked the driver for a restaurant recommendation and led Jane in the direction he'd suggested. Soon we were sitting in plastic chairs on a black sand beach with two laminated menus in our hands.

The waiter, a shirtless middle-aged man with sculpted abs and brown hair pulled into a low bun, eyed us intently as I ordered ceviche for myself and a cheese quesadilla for Jane.

"Anything for you lovely ladies. By the way, my name is Javier. I am the owner of this restaurant." He winked.

"Mucho gusto, Javier," Jane laughed shyly as he walked away.

Javier returned to our table minutes later holding two frosty glasses with little umbrellas hanging off the sides, smiling flirtatiously as he placed the drinks in front of us.

"Piña coladas on the house for you two beauties."

Jane's face flushed as she stared at the drinks, the fate of six months held in the sweating glass before her.

I should have sent the drinks back with a gracious smile and waited patiently for our food. But I thanked Javier and drew both glasses in, feeling guilt and desire for what sat before me.

"Do you mind?" I asked, the question a formality because I had already made up my mind. What I was looking for was permission to ease the shame.

"Not at all," Jane said. "Go ahead."

I took an exaggerated sip, relishing the comforting burn of rum as it slid down my throat. A mutineer on a sinking ship, I looked over at Jane—her smile vacant, her eyes a little white flag.

"I surrender," they said. I accepted her resignation as approval and quickly slurped down my drink and hers.

I should have stopped there.

But we both got drunk later that night with Javier, after he picked us up from our hostel on his ATV to bring us out dancing. I left Jane alone at a Guatemalan beach club that night, too intoxicated for loyalty and discernment, too selfish to worry about how she'd get home, instead bringing Javier back to the turtle sanctuary hostel with me.

"How old are you?" I asked as he lay on top of me, my back grinding against the sand. I wanted to feel seen, desperate for validation that I was a "good girl" when the only mouth I wanted to hear it from had been buried years ago. And so, I offered myself.

I felt so keenly alive in my destruction, in my growth and decay. It was living and dying all at once.

"Forty-four," he replied.

I woke up the next morning and Javier was gone. I rolled out of bed, relieved to see Jane in the cot beside me, and apologized for leaving her.

She smiled.

"It's okay, I had a good time!"

Jane and I spent the next week scrubbing sea turtle shells throughout the day and drinking beer around the hostel's communal table at night. We laughed and chain smoked and never talked about the pain that made us lambs to the gods that ruled us but offered ourselves up for the slaughter all the same.

At the end of our trip, on an uneventful bus ride back to Chimaltenango, we both agreed that Monterrico had been one of the best weeks of our lives. But as we lamented our return to the Mormon group with its rigid rules, I sensed that Jane was in a different kind of mourning. I recognized it because I always seemed to be an appendage to this kind of sorrow. I didn't see that it lived inside me, too.

* * *

Four days later, I was kicked out of the volunteer group. Saturated with guilt, Jane confessed our Honor Code violations to our group leader—including my night with Javier. After our leader conferred with headquarters in Utah, she and a group of elderly men made the unanimous decision to allow Jane to remain in the group due to her contrition, or for the fact that she hadn't had sex.

(*Worthy, without condition. Worthy, with condition. Unworthy.*)

When the group leader summoned me to her room to break the news, I received it with acceptance and even a little relief. I felt guilty for leading Jane astray, and this seemed like appropriate retribution, as though life was some karmic measure of discipline and reward.

As though "I deserve" held any weight in this world.

I left the Chimaltenango house before sunrise the next morning, figuring it would be easier to let the leader explain my sudden departure. I taped a group letter to the kitchen table, thanking everyone for their acceptance and love. I wrote Jane a separate note, apologizing for being such a disappointing friend, and slipped it under her pillow as she slept. I wrestled a garbage bag over my backpack, said goodbye to the puppy we had collectively adopted in another earnest attempt at unsustainably "saving" something, and walked to the bus stop in the pouring rain.

Over the weeks I had grown to love each volunteer. I was starting to see love as an undercurrent that transcended belief systems, while the wisdom of Bishop Huang's words evolved into a tangible truth: *"None of those things really matter. I see your heart. And it is good."* I began to wonder if my own insecurities had caused a sense of ethnocentricity—the very thing I vowed to abhor. Had I projected my lack of self-worth onto others? Was my critique of the world based on the myopia of self-loathing? Was my resistance to religion fostering its own judgment?

In my desire to defy the dichotomous beliefs of my childhood, perhaps I had pitted myself in an equally nearsighted worldview.

The walls I had erected around my heart, reinforced by narratives of grief and rage, were beginning to crumble. My time in Guatemala was eroding the parts of me that had been calcified by my father's death. In the rubble I was searching for the sweet girl that had been inside me all along.

Maybe we didn't have to fight.

Maybe I didn't have to choose between who I used to be and who I was becoming.

Maybe there was room for us both.

But all of these realizations were obscured by the shame I felt for being kicked out of the volunteer group. It wasn't the acts themselves that caused my shame but the embarrassment of being expelled from something that once held so much promise of *better*. As I walked alone down the Pan-American Highway, I felt the humiliation of ostracism. I started to believe that the love I felt from the volunteer group had been conditional on my actions—that my acceptance was contingent upon my adherence to a set of chalk-lined rules.

I walked to the bus stop feeling fourteen all over again, getting kicked out of a church dance because I showed up wearing ripped corduroys instead of a dress. I was sixteen and being told to wait in the parking lot while church leaders decided whether I could attend youth conference with an eyebrow ring. I was eighteen and standing outside the BYUH cafeteria because my shorts didn't quite reach my knees. I was nineteen and walking alone down a Guatemalan highway with the resounding mistruth that had been offered to me as an extension of perfection over and over again.

"You are not welcome here."

Maybe I *did* have to choose between pain and perfection, bad and better, right and wrong. Maybe there wasn't room for all of me after all.

I didn't have the heart to tell my mum I had been kicked out of the group. Instead I spent the next two weeks backpacking through Central America, sending weekly email updates about fabricated humanitarian missions when really I was snorkeling off the coast of Honduras, spending several nights in San Salvador, and riding a boat up the Rio Dulce with a group of Rastafarians to the port town of Livingston between smoky coughs.

The night before my flight home, I reserved a 3 a.m. taxi to the Greyhound station in San Pedro Sula, Honduras, for the ten-hour bus ride back to Guatemala. If everything went according to plan, I would get to the Guatemala City airport just in time for my flight back to Montreal.

The next morning, I waited outside my hostel until 3:20 a.m., but the taxi never showed. Determined to catch my bus, I walked out onto the dark streets of San Pedro Sula towards the station. After running out of money days ago, I'd had to borrow a hundred euros from a German backpacker—forty-five for the bus ticket, the rest rationed over cheap hostels, food, and beer. If I missed this bus, I would be stuck in Honduras until I could charm another drunk traveler into lending me more money. Or worse—I would have to call my mum and explain why I was alone in Honduras, 300 miles away from the volunteer group in Chimaltenango.

I trudge down the uneven roadway, my balance off kilter as a result of my overstuffed backpack and the handful of beers I consumed at the hostel bar a couple hours earlier.

A few minutes later, a man pulls up beside me in an old pickup truck.

"Very danger to walk here!" he whispers out a narrowly cracked window, motioning for me to get in. His face is gaunt, his hair a dark ponytail secured tightly against his scalp.

"Está bien!" I say with a smile and exuberant thumbs-up, my go-to response for almost everything in Central America.

"No! I take you to bus!"

He reaches over and pushes the passenger door open with an emphatic swing.

I hesitate for a moment, wondering how he knows I'm going to the bus stop before concluding that wide-eyed teenage white girls wearing patchwork linen pants and Chacos while sporting $300 The North Face backpacks down the streets of San Pedro Sula are all the same: lost and searching for home.

"Fuck it," I think. I throw my bag into the back of his truck and hop in beside him.

He looks over at me as I shut the door. His eyes are kind.

"Jesús," he says, extending his hand with a smile.

"Of course it fucking is" I want to say. Instead I shake his hand

and thank him for his kindness, offering the last few lempiras from my pocket.

"No, no money. Just cuidarse," he says, pulling up to the bus stop a few minutes later. "Please, señorita. Be careful on your way home."

I nod and thank him again before boarding the bus to Guatemala, headed for home but not knowing where to find it.

CHAPTER 13

Rivs continued to decline in the days following his intubation, now requiring 100 percent ventilator oxygen to assist with his mechanical breathing. Still undiagnosed, his lungs deteriorated as the growing nodules overwhelmed his ability to exchange oxygen and carbon dioxide. His oxygenation was further compromised as his body fought against the ventilator in autonomic defiance. Even when unconscious, Rivs's fight could not be turned off.

"He keeps moving around no matter what we do," a nurse said during an update call on day five of his sedation. "We've administered more sedatives than I've ever seen a patient receive and he's still pulling at his tubes."

Then, like a confession, she whispered, "Last night we had to put him in restraints," her voice hushed as though she, too, recognized the irony of Rivs strapped to a bed. Or anyone strapped to a bed, for that matter.

You stubborn motherfucker, I thought once again, sickened by the idea of Rivs tied down. I hung up the phone and sat on our front porch, sobbing desolate tears and floundering in the newness of feeling it all.

I had spent years hiding from my emotions. I'd grown distant from my feelings, believing myself to be truly stoic, just like my mother. I'd moved through life seemingly unaffected by sadness and stress. "I'm fine, just fine," I'd say with a smile if anyone ever asked, just like my mother, not realizing that my impassive countenance was the very thing I had resented about her throughout my adolescence.

Not realizing that detachment was not a virtue but a defense.

Confronting Rivs's mortality brought my sorrow into plain view. As his sedation wore on, the memories I had been avoiding all my life coursed through my veins in pushes of nostalgic grief. There was no more muting them, no more drowning them, no more covering them up.

Tragedy had sanded me down. Opened me up. Left me raw and exposed.

Maybe it had been the same for Mum. Maybe she hurt too deeply to allow herself to feel it all. Maybe she couldn't allow herself to scratch the surface of her own exquisite pain because it was all just *too much.*

Like her, I didn't know how to feel it all because I'd always been taught I had to choose between sadness and joy, sin and perfection, happiness and despair, pain and perfection. And maybe, unlike me, she hadn't been extended the grace I'd been given to try and fail over and over again.

Now sadness seeped through me. It consumed me. It changed me on a cellular level, and I atrophied in darkness. How could I do this all over again? How could I lead my children down a path I was still forging for myself? How could I possibly feel it all?

The terror was pathological. I could barely see a way out.

Barely.

But here it was, rising over the horizon in the most unlikely time— a glimmer of my strength emitted through a voice I couldn't explain. On the darkest days I saw my own light, grounded by the love surrounding me.

This is not how he dies.

I remembered the voice and understood what it represented: Resolve. Action.

Having been so gravely disappointed by expectation in the past, could I widen my gaze past the rational? Could I reach for hope once more?

I struggled with this choice, aware that the fall from its height was a pulley system with no counterweight. The ballast had been emptied long ago. If I leapt, my landing might be a deafening thud, like little Phil on the ground below our treehouse. I was terrified about what pieces of me would be broken if hope turned into another shattering lie. Still, I couldn't deny the truth I felt when the voice shook me that night.

This is not how he dies.

I took a running jump. I reached for it. I believed.

This is not how he dies.

This hope remained the next day, when I was told that it was finally time to visit Rivs in the ICU. Aware that this invitation indicated Rivs was nearing end-of-life status, I was eager to see him. Desperate, even.

It was eighteen days before that I had dropped him at the ER and rushed a masked kiss on his cheek. Now I wanted to touch his face with intention—to feel the warmth of his skin and marvel at the miracle of it. I wanted to weigh his silence against my father's and gauge for myself just how close death was hovering.

I drove to the hospital aware of every breath, the thinness of each exhale a drawn-out echo of uncertainty. I was headed towards the space between life and death. What was I going to find this time?

I parked the car and walked on shaking legs into the hospital, the quiet of its visitor-less reception only adding to my fear. I was met at the hospital entrance by a kind security guard who led me down hallways that were silent despite the heartbreak and horror behind each lonely door. Because what words could ever honor the marriage of hope and fear? What could possibly be said in the space between them?

I walked towards the ICU, past faceless nurses in bright yellow PPE gear who shuffled between rooms in exhausted reverence. Theirs was a countenance I knew well—one that pleaded for life while being careful not to offend death. I knew, because that's how we walked around Dad's room towards the end—our arms folded, our heads bowed, our mouths not knowing whether to scream in anger or beg in prayer, but unequivocally humbled by watching the end of a whole life.

Weren't you just right here?

I navigated the hospital halls with both hands clutching a small bag of things Rivs couldn't enjoy anymore—Powerade, Nutter Butters, Breathe Right strips, Tapatío—each one a symbol of resistance against mortality or a reminder of the things he might never hold again. Or maybe I brought them because the finality of absence takes years to reckon. Sometimes tokens of an imagined presence keep us going, like the rose left on Dad's empty bed or how Mum kept the applesauce on his tray table long after he was gone.

(Weren't you just right here?)

The only visitor allowed in the ICU that week, the nurses all recognized me as I approached their small congregation of desks. I could feel them commiserate in unspoken condolence as I waved to greet them, their empathy only adding to the gravity of my visit. For the first time I was grateful for the pandemic's necessity of masks and goggles. Seeing the pain in their eyes would have broken me completely. Luckily, it wasn't long before Rivs's nurse, Tara, welcomed me with warmth.

"What a difficult time to have a loved one in the hospital," she said, snapping on a fresh pair of gloves as she prepared to escort me to his room. "I'm so sorry you have to be here, sweetie, but I'm so glad you are. I wish I could hug you."

"Me too. Thank you for everything you've done for him." It was a trite thing to say to the person wringing themselves dry for my husband, but it was all I had.

"Oh, please don't thank me. We all love Rivs so much."

I followed next to her in clumsy steps, my legs quivering as we walked down a narrow corridor accompanied by a muted chorus of beeps and alarms. Along the way, Tara told me about how when Rivs was awake she'd spent hours sitting by his bed, talking about life and mulling over the mystery of his unexplained illness. She even pretended not to watch whenever he'd slip off his oxygen monitor to do quick sets of pushups during the early days of his hospitalization.

"That man's will to live is unparalleled. Caring for him over the past few weeks has truly made an impact on my life."

I nodded my head in agreement. Once Rivs let you in, it was almost impossible not to love him. To not be changed by him. I was comforted by knowing that he was being cared for by someone who loved him like that, someone he'd let in. Someone he'd allowed himself to love back.

Finally, we stopped in front of what I assumed to be Rivs's room, though it was unremarkable other than the knowledge that it was his. I thought about how many things are unremarkable until they're taken away from us as Tara pulled a yellow medical gown from a metal cart and handed it to me.

"Now, the rules are that you can touch him, you can talk to him, you can even kiss him . . . just not on the face!" she advised as I tried to suit up despite my trembling hands.

I nodded, my heart beating so forcefully I could feel it in my ears, the fragile strands holding me together fraying from both ends as I came closer to seeing him.

I didn't know how to prepare myself. Should I tell him to keep fighting, strong and resolute? Or was I there to offer peace, to say goodbye in a series of calculated whispers? I didn't know. I don't think anyone ever does until they're in the thick of it. And even then, probably not.

Sensing my fear, Tara grabbed my wrist with a gloved hand and gave it a squeeze. I could feel her warmth even through the layers separating our skin. I let her hold me, appreciating the permeability of love.

"Also . . ." Her eyes widened in concern. "I want to tell you something very important that I . . . well . . . all the nurses have been talking about."

I smiled behind my mask and nodded again, too nervous for words.

"When the doctor comes in, you need to ask questions. You need to write them down when you're sitting next to Rivs today, then corner the doctor in the room. Ask him everything that's on your mind. Don't let him leave until he's answered every one of them. Okay?"

"Okay," I said, trying to hide the tears fogging up my safety goggles, thinking that Rivs and I would probably be laughing together at the sight of it if he were here. And then I remembered that he *was* here, and how strange it is to be both here and nowhere.

"The doctors need to know that you're still fighting for him. They need to believe that he still has a chance. You need to show them that *you* still believe he still has a chance."

I shivered. Again, it felt like too much—the responsibility of life resting on my shoulders, the survival of it contingent upon my ability to be assertive and confrontational. I had felt a sliver of my strength but still didn't know how to channel it. Standing in front of his door, I felt completely helpless.

And then: *This is not how he dies.*

"Okay, Tara. Okay. I will."

Tara took my hand in her own, the warmth still there. I turned and stood in front of his room feeling like a child.

"You ready?"

I took a deep breath, reminding myself that I'd been here before, in front of this room. I had been a child standing before life and death, unsure of what I'd find on the other side. And there was something oddly comforting about this—knowing I could stand here forever and never be ready.

"Yes."

Tara opened the door to a stuffy, windowless room that was now an entire universe. And there he was, lying on his back, his head propped with pillows, tubes going into his nose and down his throat, his tongue hanging from his mouth, his wrists tied to the bed, there he was. This monolith of a man, swollen with interstitial fluid, strapped down and motionless other than the robotic breaths that jerked his body in an unnatural rhythm.

I stood there staring. I couldn't move.

It was only four weeks ago, while the girls were away with Julie, that we'd spent hours running through the forest together, giggling like little kids and marveling at the beauty of the forest.

In the middle of the trail Rivs stops to comment on the integrity of the natural world, how nothing is random or unremarkable even though it sometimes seems that way. "Maybe life is like that," he says. "Maybe meaning is our own to make."

Then he blows a giant bubble with his watermelon Hubba Bubba gum, and the pop makes us stumble with laughter. We don't think much about how hard he pulls for each inhale, how he struggles to keep up as we run.

"Maybe I'm just tired. Or maybe it's just hard getting back into shape," he says.

"Remember, he can hear you," Tara whispered, breaking me from the memory and leading me into his room. "Even if it doesn't seem like it, he can always hear you."

At that moment I loved no one more than her—a stranger willing to walk me into the unknown.

I studied the room's anemic walls and their matching floor, trying to ignore how much his room felt like a closet—like it wasn't meant for someone who was going to come out alive. Tara gave me one last squeeze before closing the door behind her, leaving me alone in the space between life and death I would come to know so well. And he looked like that—caught in between. At first I'd thought he looked helpless and defeated, but the longer I stood there, the more I could sense his presence. Somehow, despite the trauma of seeing him splayed out on the hospital bed in the same outdated hospital gown my father had once worn, I knew there was life left inside him.

In this room, death wasn't close and I wasn't alone. I could *feel* it. Though it defied science and empirical evidence and everything I had previously believed to be true, I was certain that somewhere in this bleak and fiery space, Rivs was fighting. Hard.

As I walked towards him, each step became less tentative than the next. It felt like I was crossing worlds to get there, carried by love and a memory.

This is not how he dies.

Traveling across the universe I reached for him. The closer I came, the less scared I was. My heart stopped racing. My legs steadied.

This is not how he dies.

I pulled a chair next to his bed and eased into the mechanical movement of his breathing. I became less distraught over the tubes going in and out of his body. Through it all, I knew it was still him. I could feel him through it all.

"Hey, babe," I said, my voice finding itself as I unwrapped the Velcro from his arm restraints, trying to free him just a bit before nestling my hand under his. In some way I wanted to pretend that he'd reached for me, that he'd lifted his hand and placed it on mine.

I was comforted by his touch despite the tautness of skin stretched to its limit. A nurse later told me that most critically ill patients experience edema due to the body's inability to excrete intravenous hydration while immobile, but *puffy and distorted* was how it looked to me. It was so unlike my dad's cold hand when I'd touched his lifeless skin all those years ago.

I remember thinking what an odd word it was to describe Rivs—*immobile*—when his whole life had been built on mobility. I thought about how my dad had never been *cold* a day in his life—he had been a beacon of warmth and welcome. I thought about how finite descriptors are, how fleetingly we claim ourselves, how it can all be taken away in an instant, how impermanence denoted the imperative of *now*.

I sat with Rivs the entire day. Immersed in the purity of presence, it felt as though time was standing still, like we were being held in a sacred place not of this world. Despite the sterility of his room and the tragedy of our circumstance, everything felt warm. I talked to him, listened to music, played recordings of our daughters' voices, and sat in revered silence. I held him as close as I could from my plastic chair and tried my best to wade through the abstruse, to channel all the love I could summon from me, the girls, and the world to him.

By the time Dr. Hemmerman entered the room nine hours later, I had gathered the courage to ask my questions, the hardest being "do you think he's going to survive?"

"At this point we just don't know. I'm sorry." Dr. Hemmerman looked at the ground as though the words were an embarrassing admission. "With undiagnosed lung injuries, it can go either way. So far, Tommy hasn't been responding to treatment. He is on day two of high dose corticosteroids and a strong antifungal medication. Right now, we are not seeing any improvement. Unfortunately, he is continuing to decline."

"But what do *you* think? Do you think he's going to live?" It took all the bravery I could find.

"I—I don't know. I wish I could say." He continued to look down, submitting to uncertainty—the nemesis of medicine. "I'm sorry, but it doesn't look good. We don't know what else to do for him. Without a diagnosis, there's nothing more we *can* do. I really am sorry."

Then he hurried out of the room leaving me alone once more, though it felt much less lonely than when I'd first arrived.

Tara led me out of the ICU an hour later. Before leaving, she whispered in Rivs's ear, just loud enough for me to hear.

"I better see you on my next shift, Rivs. That's two days, my friend. Two days. Okay?"

I left the hospital ready to accept the medical reality Dr. Hemmerman had presented to me. I didn't want to be full of hope only to be blindsided, but something was pulling me away from logic. Perhaps I was simply clinging to words of equivocation in an act of self-preservation: "so far," "we don't know," "I wish." Or maybe it was something deeper causing my mounting sense of hope as I left Rivs's side that night.

As I drove home, I thought about the unscientific nature of dismissing truth solely based on its disputability. I wondered how many truths I had discounted in my life since my father's death, in my sterile view of the world. I decided that sometimes, in the attempt to be open minded, we close ourselves off from the rich and varying realities that surround us.

I pulled into my driveway and decided that intuition is sometimes more reliable than fact.

Tonight I would choose hope.

And that hope remained the next day, when the hospital chaplain called to ask whether he could offer peace as Rivs "transitioned" from this earth.

"Would it be okay if I offered my version of faith to your husband as he nears the end of this life?"

That hope remained, though wavering, when his night nurse informed me later that evening that he might not make it through the night. His oxygen was declining despite maximum ventilator settings. The time had come to place him on his stomach in a prone position, as they had started to do with critical COVID-19 patients in respiratory distress, but they were unsure whether he would survive the rotation, and would I consent to the procedure?

That hope remained, though distant, after I consented on his behalf and hung up the phone. I ran into the forest as the sun was setting, crying at the trees in unresolved rage and dissonant sorrow, feeling it all at once—hope and defeat, love and loss, anger and gratitude, grieving wife and grieving child.

"They said he might die tonight," I sobbed through the phone to Rachel as I ran through the sprouting oak and craggy juniper ablaze in the sun's lowering rays. My sister had become my best friend over the years, far removed from the days I used to stumble into her LA home drunk and defiant.

"H—hhhow?" she stammered, still believing that grief had a lifetime measure.

"I don't know, Ray. I don't know . . . What do I tell the girls? I can't do it, Ray. I don't think I can do it."

It is a unique hell to understand the significance of your children's pain. To be the daughter of a dying father was an abyss. I didn't want my daughters to be shielded and shocked by reality, but I didn't want them to live in fear, either. It was then, in the loneliness of heartbreak, that I felt overwhelming gratitude for having lived through my father's sickness.

Just as my mother was the only one in my life who truly understood what I was going through, so was I for my three daughters. What a unique hell, but also, what a unique gift to have been here before. How tragic it is to know we see others best through pain.

Meaning is our own to make, I thought as I held my head in my hands and sobbed years-long tears on the forest floor while Mum and Julie held my daughters at home.

(It's okay, it's okay, it's okay.)

* * *

I wrestled sleep that night, overcome by gratitude and sorrow. I was tormented by the knowledge that I might be called at any moment to say goodbye, though I was certain Rivs was still fighting. Just as I'd come to experience the palpable space between life and death where he now lived, I knew there was a merger between hope and reason. I knew that truth rested in the balance. I just needed to find it.

I finally dozed off in the early hours and woke to the alarm I had set to call the night nurse during her morning shift change. I cried with relief when she said that his body was holding steady. He was no better, but no worse. In the night they had decided against proning when a blood draw found him in "extreme hypercapnia," which meant he had near-fatal levels of carbon dioxide in his blood. His body was too critical for movement. Instead, they had raised the volume settings on his ventilator, which increased the pressure of oxygen entering his lungs and helped sweep out some excess carbon dioxide from his blood.

I sat up in bed, careful not to wake Iris, who had been sleeping next to me every night since the beginning of Rivs's hospitalization. Sipping the coffee Mum had rushed to bring me upon hearing the buzz of my alarm, I started researching last-resort care for lung disease.

In my online search it was quickly apparent that the only viable therapy left for him was extracorporeal membrane oxygenation, or ECMO—a life support device that extracted hypoxic blood from the body through large catheters placed in the jugular vein and right aorta. That blood was then spun through a machine, pumping in oxygen and sweeping out excess carbon dioxide before being put back into the body at a constant rate. By literal definition, it was having lungs outside of the body.

I had never heard of ECMO before but the more I looked into it, the more promising it felt despite its high-risk factor, with a mortality rate of 52 percent. Unsure whether the Flagstaff hospital even *had* ECMO resources, I was now determined to ask. As the ventilator was failing to support Rivs's lungs, it seemed like his only chance of survival.

The time to be passive was over. I could no longer defer to others— not to Rivs, not to a god, not to chance. If he was going to survive, I knew I had to reach inside and find my own voice. It was time to trust myself.

I needed to make my presence known to forces seen and unseen.

More than anything, I needed to let my presence be known to me.

This is not how he dies.

CHAPTER 14

I thought about ecstasy the whole time I was in Guatemala. It wasn't so much the feeling I craved but the sense of freedom and acceptance it proffered.

I dreamed about it.

I chased it through a revolving door of desire and guilted liberation.

I was hunting for peace not knowing how to sustain it on my own, not seeing that my methods of attaining it were fleeting and always demanding of more, more, more.

I didn't see that tiny blue pills were never happiness but simply pain interrupted.

After leaving Central America, I went back to Montreal so determined to get high that I ended up snorting mystery drugs from a stranger in a bathroom stall at an after-hours club with Marc, my best friend from high school.

Marc and I had been inseparable since meeting the day after Dad's death, when I went to school hoping to carry on as normal. Mum begged me to stay home but I insisted on going, the thought of Shakespeare and algebra far more welcoming than spending the day in a newly fatherless family.

I didn't want to tell anyone at school that he had died, but somehow everyone already knew.

My walk to class is a montage of weeping teenagers wanting to take part in a sorrow I am unwilling to share. I'm not ready to let empathy validate his absence as I squeeze through the crowd of well-meaning students, though I tender a smile until the first bell rings. Comforted by a sound that normally induces dread, I slump against my locker as the halls grow silent. Pulling my backpack onto my lap like a shield, I resign myself to a day of unwelcome condolences.

I am debating whether to make my way to homeroom class or sneak out the back door when I hear the unmistakable squeak of Vans on linoleum. I keep my eyes down, hoping the approaching feet belong to a wayward eleventh grader on their way to sneak a cigarette and not another acquaintance sharing their commiseration. The illusion fades when I feel the shuffling stop a few meters away from me. My eyes glued to the floor, I feel the feet hovering in front of me.

I look up to see Marc. His face is familiar from the back of ninth grade English class, where people hiss homophobic slurs as he walks past the rows of relentless teens.

He stands before me in silence, pulling at the sleeve of a sweatshirt that hangs loosely on his overweight frame. He is nervous, though a warm smile is stretched across his acne-riddled cheeks.

He clears his throat.

"Hey, it's my dad's birthday. Do you want to get out of here?"

I smirk at his ill-timed proposition before responding "fuck yes." Mired in an actionable pain that denotes awareness, something about Marc feels like home. It is one of those tangible truths I can feel but never explain.

Marc and I take the city bus to buy a Betty Crocker cake mix before going back to his house to bake and laugh and never once mention my dad.

Five years later, we conspired against pain in a Montreal night club bathroom stall.

When the drugs took off that night, I knew something was off. My heart raced, my palms sweat, my mind shook seismically without the rolling elation that normally accompanied the soft high of MDMA. I looked over at Marc, who was scratching at his skin uncomfortably.

Less than an hour later he was racing me to the hospital. If ever I needed a love story this was it: my dead father, a Betty Croker cake mix, my rising grief, my tweaking best friend, and his tender hands clenched on the steering wheel like my life depended on it.

Because maybe it did.

The sun was summitting the high rises as Marc sped down the waking streets, its light cruelly illuminating a city that held far too many memories of my innocence.

And somewhere between the drugs, the fear, the hands, the wheel, the light around my homesick city, I broke. The levy gave way. With nothing to divert the current, the flood was far more powerful than the anger stonewalled before it. After years of hiding behind my fortress of rage, my sorrow was finally breached.

It was so simple. For the first time, I remembered my father. For the first time, I missed him.

It was sadness all along.

Speeding down the streets of early morning rush hour I saw myself— a little girl stunted by sorrow, desperate to feel nothing and pleading for anything to take everything else away.

I looked at Marc and tried to make a joke, to express anything other than this. I opened my mouth to change the subject but a sob came out instead, deep and loud and guttural. Marc reached over and grabbed my hand, anchoring me when it felt like all my pieces were floating away.

Because the right kind of love is just that—an anchor.

Together we cried tears of years-long sorrow, tears that united us despite our distinct trauma stories. Flowing over the keys of grief, we held each other above time and space in the unspoken universality of pain.

All of these years we had been too afraid to be soft, our truths too painful to be expressed. All the words we'd ever been called, all the lies we'd ever believed about ourselves were now right in front of us, bright as the dawning sun: *fag, punk, slut, delinquent, whore, sinner, disappointment.*

We cried together all the way to the hospital, heavy tears that had been hiding behind an indolent fear. The dam of rage eroded beyond containment, and I now knew my brokenness. Held by the purity of Marc's love, I was free to collapse.

"Hi. I think I'm . . . dying?" I said to the ER receptionist without a hint of facetiousness after Marc dropped me at the hospital entrance. Before he'd even parked, I was triaged and labeled as a sullen teen with an amphetamine-induced panic attack.

Other than copious amounts of methamphetamine in my blood and a case of moderate dehydration, there was nothing physiologically wrong with me.

"There must be some mistake. Can't you see I'm dying?" I cried to the nurse, because that's how it felt, an all-consuming sadness that would surely swallow me whole.

"You'll be fine. Just stop hurting yourself," she responded while finding a cooperative vein for an IV.

Before leaving my curtained hospital stall, she glanced at my chart with a mix of sympathy and consternation.

"You're nineteen years old, sweetheart. You're too young to be here with this poison in your body."

"I didn't mean for any of this to be in my body," I wanted to say.

But I nodded my head in agreement and reached for Marc, who was resting his head on the metal rail of my hospital bed. When he looked up, I could see an indentation of the rail grooved into his round cheek. I laughed.

"Let's be better," I said, still groping for what it meant but hoping that perhaps this was the beginning of it.

"Let's be better," he said back.

It was midday when I walked out of the hospital into broad daylight with a prescription for Xanax in my hand and Marc by my side, the sun scorching our eyes. We ran to the car holding each other, alternating between weeping and laughter as we screamed "my retinas are burning!" into the air.

We cried and giggled the whole way home, professing our platonic love for each other and vowing to never do drugs ever, *ever* again. It was then that I started to understand the truth of the little brown buildings in LA and Guatemala, and the gracious humility that accompanied acceptance.

It was less about submitting to a higher power, and more about accepting the suffering that made us who we are.

Cushioned by Marc's unfaltering friendship, I was safe to feel my brokenness. In many ways I was saved by Marc's love—one that was extended without condition or the expectation that he would make me whole. In turn, Marc held a mirror to the inherent goodness inside me, even when I was unable to recognize it. To be loved by Marc was to be seen without presumption. Held in the hazed reflection of my worth, I was free to start accepting myself.

* * *

Two weeks after my brief hospital visit, I experienced depression for the first time.

It started with a hollow whisper, an ominous feeling of emptiness that lingered in my chest. I went to bed each night begging for the feeling to pass. I called out to the god of my childhood, as though I could leverage omnipotence, as though life was a bottle that could be filled with a limited amount of sorrow, the rest benevolently absorbed by deity or absolved by good works. Once again I was searching for a power outside myself to save me, but the lifeline was never thrown.

Here was sorrow in all its wrath, taking over me so wholly as though to make up for the years of lost time. Each morning I awoke to the same voice in my ear. It spoke with malice, equipped with the scriptural vocabulary of my youth.

"You deserve this, you are vile and wretched, this is the life you've sown, now you reap the consequence of sin."

Eventually the emptiness was a pair of hands moving from my chest to my throat. I was choked by it, but there was no way to loosen its grip. Like an unspoken truth, the more I tried to push it away, the tighter it held me. It was debilitating, a total consuming of my being, extinguishing any sense of self I might have held on to over the years.

I tried to remember the idea of me, but without the guise of anger and its accompanying recklessness, I no longer knew who I was. I didn't know how to be sad. I felt like a bystander in my own life, going through the motions while being smothered by despair.

In an attempt to mute the feeling, I filled my days with friends and distractions. I worked long hours as a landscaper alongside my brother Dave—mowing lawns and laying sod in twelve-hour shifts, accompanied only by his kind encouragement and a Discman that played Pink Floyd on repeat.

> *I cannot put my finger on it now*
> *The child is grown*
> *The dream is gone*
> *(. . .)*
> *I have become comfortably numb*

I was afraid to be alone with my mind as I reconciled who I used to be with the "better" self I was hoping to become. In the silence, all I felt was torment.

One afternoon, Marc and I bought a live lobster from the grocery store in an attempt to emancipate the trapped creature from its tank, but it died in my bathtub a few hours later. It was only as the lobster's lifeless claw waved up at us from under its freshwater bath that we remembered that lobsters were saltwater creatures.

"Well, fuck," Marc muttered as we scooped it from its death pool, disappointed by yet another display of mis-intention.

Later that day, determined to send the lobster off with a penitent farewell, we made a parachute from a plastic grocery bag and drove to a ravine to throw it off the cliff with some eulogistic words. Despite our anticipation of a graceful fall, we watched its limp body plummet into the rocks below, the grocery bag doing little to bolster its landing.

"Well, fuck!" Marc said once again as we laughed at the darkness of it all.

But later that night I fantasized about jumping off a cliff with a garbage bag parachute. To feel the merciless polarity I'd been raised to believe in.

Mum tried her best to help, but my sadness scared her. With noble intentions she'd knock on my bedroom door to offer words of encouragement as I lay cocooned in blankets, paralyzed by anxiety. For the life of her she didn't understand why I couldn't just snap out of it.

"Just think happy thoughts!" she'd cheer from the doorway, a delivery of homemade muffins in her hands. And I'd smile, wishing it was that easy while having already learned that mental illness did not negotiate with sanguine desires or positive affirmations. I'd felt its unassailable pull. I knew that optimism had no authority here.

But by the end of summer, her words had changed.

"I'm so sorry. I should have brought you to therapy when Dad died."

Now I recognize the words she never said.

I'm so sorry. I thought I could carry it all.

* * *

It was late August when I boarded the plane back to Oahu for the fall semester, clutching a bottle of Xanax in one hand and my Book of Mormon in the other—my weapons against despair. I flew over the Pacific Ocean resolved to be a good Mormon, hoping once again that *better* might be found in subservience and laws of abstinence, and that happiness might be found somewhere therein.

Over the weeks I had come back to the damaging conclusion that my mental illness was divine punishment for my sins—that life was a dogmatic meritocracy where righteous actions begot blessings and sinful acts begot sorrow and punishment. In my youth I had been taught that true joy was only found inside the LDS church—that if I left the fold, I would never again feel real happiness. Now, I was beginning to believe it was true.

I started rereading the Book of Mormon, writing in my notebook any passage that offered solace, the very same notebook that held desperate prayers for my ailing father. I trusted that piety would exorcise the hopelessness that possessed me—just as I had believed it would heal my father. In desperation I thought that perfection would make me whole.

Intent on forging yet another new path for myself in Hawaii, I moved into a plywood island shack seven miles from campus in a small town called Punaluʻu. My only neighbor was a forty-five-year-old Hawaiian man named Solomon who had just been released from prison after a five-year sentence for robbery. My roommates were a lesbian couple who had to hide their relationship far from the BYUH campus, where their love wasn't welcome.

I loved that house nestled against the lush Koʻolau mountain range, with its wild chickens and boisterous peacocks that ran between the palm trees in our yard, waking us up long before sunrise. My bed was a blow-up mattress on the floor and my window was a gaping hole in the wall with a Bob Marley sarong slung over it, always billowing wide open despite my feeble attempt at privacy. When it rained, I'd sometimes put a garbage bag over the space, but usually I'd just move my bed over so it wouldn't get wet.

I grew quiet and introverted throughout the semester. I spent mornings in the classroom and afternoons on the beach with my Book of Mormon in one hand, a pen and notebook in the other. I was digging for answers, desperate to assign divine reason to my suffering. I believed that obedience and depression were purifying fires in whose crucible I'd eventually be made whole. This was another damaging notion I had been taught in church—that "enduring" was a rite of passage to perfection, that being a martyr to despair was a hallmark of eternal worth and redemption. If I could emerge from this hell relieved of my sins, my depression would have been worth it.

During this time my closest friend was a pit bull puppy I found soaking wet and shivering under a banyan tree next to my favorite surf spot. I named her Kava. Having something to care for made me feel a little less hopeless and a lot less lonely.

I remained devout and sober for months, stagnant in my mental progression but convinced that I was moving forward through penance and obedience. When Kava died, everything changed.

I was typing a cultural studies essay in my room when I heard screeching tires and the gut-wrenching thump of flesh on metal. I ran to the door, only then realizing that the screen had been left open. I hurried to the street to see Kava lying lifeless in the road, her innocent mouth curled open in a form all too familiar. I tried scooping her up but buckled to my knees. Weakened by panic, I couldn't lift her. I bent my head and wept.

Then a pair of hands reach out beside me. They are lifting Kava's body from the ground. I look up to see Solomon, shirtless and potbellied with a cigarette pinched between his lips, absorbing what I can't sustain. Together we carry Kava home, our arms sharing the weight of her body. We lay her in my yard. Solomon turns and limps back home, his short frame hunched forward in a manner that denotes years of pain, or manual labor, or both. He emerges from his front door just moments later with a grin on his face and a rusted shovel in his hand. Without saying a word, he stands beside me and starts digging a shallow grave.

Rain breaks the dusky sky as he hands me the shovel and asks me to throw a final scoop of dirt over her body. When it is done, he looks over the mound and offers a bent cigarette from the pocket of his boardshorts, shielding it from the rain with a worn hand.

I accept it. We stand next to each other smoking in silence, looking over Kava in the ground and sharing the unspoken understanding that everything we love will eventually be buried or already has been. The sun has long retreated behind the mountains when Solomon puts his arm around me like a father, saying some words about the circle of life in thick Hawaiian pidgin.

"Stay hea, sistah," he says before running back to his house once more. He returns minutes later, this time with a six-pack of beer tucked under his arm and a couple of plastic lawn chairs in his hands. He hands me a lukewarm can and positions the chairs side by side in front of Kava's fresh grave.

I crack open the warm Coors Light and cheers Solomon. I haven't had a drink in almost a year—not since the hospital with Marc, not since sorrow, shame, and fear have choked off any room for release.

But this is my first experience with death since my dad. I am unsure where it fits on the spectrum of better, but tonight, drinking a warm beer with Solomon feels right.

For the first time since his death, I think about burying my dad. I remember how the pallbearers cried so hard they had to set his coffin down. How Phil hid his face in my lap when we sat in the church pews and didn't lift it until the funeral was over. How I didn't shed a single tear as we stood together in the autumn wind while they lowered Dad's casket into the ground.

I've tried to explain my depression as divine retribution, but it was grief all along. There is no eternal weight to it. I've fought against the acknowledgment of my sorrow with countless excuses, time and time again. But it is so simple.

My dad is dead, and I am sad.

I sat next to Solomon well into the night, smoking cigarettes and crying and laughing and drinking warm beer, listening to his prison stories and tales of growing up parentless and alone, telling him about how my dad used to throw me into the lake from the dock of our cottage in upstate New York, or how he would bring me flowers and take me to Red Lobster for popcorn shrimp, or how he would chase me around the house and put me in a giant pot on the stove, saying he was going to make Steph stew.

That night I thought about betterness and decided that Solomon was the best person I knew. I went to sleep harnessed by a peculiar feeling—one I hadn't felt in a long time.

It was a glimpse of peace, and not the fleeting kind. Held in the purity of Solomon's love, once again I saw myself.

In the weeks that followed, I tried to maintain a relationship with the god I had been taught as a child, but never felt his presence in buildings and books. In truth, I never had. In all of my devotion, nothing felt truer than Solomon. No love held more salvation than Marc's. No hands held more benevolence than Solomon's. The church taught that I had to humble myself to truly know god, but depression had brought me to my knees so emphatically that I didn't think I could sink any lower. I started to question why a loving god would want me on my knees, anyway.

It became more plausible that god was a hand reached across the worn seats of a hatchback Honda Civic. God was the moonlight gleaming off the calm ocean on a clear night. God was a pair of worn hands lifting a dead dog off broken asphalt.

God was not a man. God was an act. A feeling.

* * *

I meet Rivs in anthropology class a few months later. I am about to turn twenty-two and have just weaned myself off a round of antide-pressants when he walks past my desk. Everything about him grabs my attention, from his strong jawline and kind eyes to the pinstripe overalls and paperboy hat he wears with quiet confidence.

He reaches into his backpack to remove a bag of pretzels and a large container of hummus while the professor starts the lecture. His hands are big and worn, but I notice a tenderness to them as he splays out his snacks. I observe the way his hummus is sealed with a sheet of tinfoil, perfectly taut. There is a gentleness to him, tentative but sincere. I can see it from across the room. Perhaps feeling the pull of my stare, Rivs glances over at me. When I look into his eyes, there is something familiar about him. In his stare is a memory.

Something I've always known to be true.

He gives a subtle smile before dipping a pretzel in hummus and popping it into his mouth.

"I remember you," I think before looking away.

We are married a year later.

CHAPTER 15

It had been fifteen years since I buried Kava, twenty since burying my dad, when I was confronted with the possibility of burying Rivs at the age of thirty-five. Over the decades, my idea of god ebbed and flowed, undulating between staunch atheism and transitory spirituality, though I never returned to the notion of a celestial founding father. As Rivs's death became a medical certainty, I wondered whether I'd resort to prayer in desperation like I had for my father, knowing that we pan for meaning in familiar places when hope sifts through the cracks.

I wondered whether the recognition of my own power would be enough to root me in the evanescence between life and death, or if my need for comfort would lead me to search outside myself for strength once more. Would the voice continue to guide me, or would I have to look for it in hidden places, with arms folded on bent knees as I'd been taught as a child? Did divine inspiration come from meekness or in the proprietorship of my own strength? Would my fear of the finality of death guide me to a practice that had once so starkly failed me?

These questions would be answered in auxiliary to my only priority: keeping Rivs alive.

I was now determined to get him on ECMO. Without a diagnosis I knew that a clear way forward was impossible, but I was resolute that he wouldn't go without one final display of his life's defining characteristic.

Together we needed to push the limits.

I continued my research on ECMO while Julie and Mum took the girls on a hike to see Flagstaff's wildflowers which, by late July, were in full bloom. As our daughters ran through fields illuminated by rustling hues of purple, red, and gold, I learned that only certain hospitals offered ECMO and its accompanying team of specialists. Because the Flagstaff hospital was not an ECMO center, Rivs's only chance of survival was to be transferred to a different facility. This was a mortally weighted choice given his unstable condition, and one I'd be offered only if we found a medical team willing to accept him into their care.

As I would learn, ECMO was a device reserved only as a bridge to recovery for those with a high likelihood of survival. These qualifying parameters were further tightened during the pandemic due to a national shortage of ECMO resources. As far as the doctors in Flagstaff were concerned, Rivs had little hope of crossing any bridge to relative health. In fact, it was beginning to look like there wasn't a bridge for him at all. This was why they hadn't presented me with the option of transfer, even when the ventilator was failing to support his life. His lungs were so compromised by lesions and inflammation that no one would accept him for care at a different facility.

Early afternoon on July 23 my phone rang, the ringtone seared into my mind as deep as the fear that accompanied its foreboding trill. Rachel had just walked through my front door, her ash-blond hair a stringy mess from having flown in on a red-eye.

With her carry-on bag still hung from her shoulder, Rachel marched through our home and straight out the sliding back doors, where I was pacing around the backyard, trying to steady my breath as the doctor greeted me from the other end of the line. Rachel held me in a warm embrace and I melted in her arms.

"Hello Stephanie, this is Dr. Avril, one of your husband's ICU pulmonologists."

"Hi," I said, because what else can be said to the herald of death?

"I wanted to tell you that the biopsy results are in."

"Okay," I submitted, because surrender is sometimes easier than battling through an impassive trench of denial. Sometimes.

"The good news is that we have an official diagnosis from the Mayo Clinic."

The world stuttered. At once time was both violent and still, stammering in knowing I didn't want to know because knowing would make it real. If having a diagnosis was the good news, I wasn't sure I could handle the bad. I handed the phone to Rachel, wanting to hear the determinative words from someone I loved rather than someone I'd never met—to make it real in person.

Rachel took the phone from my hand, her face twisting as she held it to her ear, her lips stretched flat as though silence might change the outcome. I knew the allure of *what if*, of wondering whether the course of tragedy might have been different had certain words not been spoken, how a single sentence could extend or end a life.

"Ray, just tell me."

She hesitated a moment, her eyes on the ground as she lowered the phone. Another *what if* before looking at me in agony. Then she let out a single, stifled sob before nodding her head as if to admit defeat to the course laid before us, understanding as well as me that all the *what ifs* in the world would never change what she was about to say.

Twenty-one days after his admission to the hospital, we finally had Rivs's diagnosis.

"Extranodal natural killer (NK)/T-cell lymphoma. It's stage IV lung cancer. Steph . . . it's terminal. There's nothing they can do."

"Okay," I said. "Okay."

"I'm so sorry, Steph."

"No, it's okay. It's really okay."

And somehow it was, though this time it wasn't surrender I felt; it was nostalgia.

Because it was cancer. I knew it well. There was something strangely comforting about fighting a familiar disease despite its grave prognosis.

I'd slept beside my baby brother on nauseous nights of chemotherapy and had laid wet washcloths on my father's forehead when radiation caused his searing headaches. I had listened to my older brother's clandestine plan for testicular cancer surgery at the age of twenty-one without letting Mum know, under the guise of being out of town for a wakeboard competition so she wouldn't worry. I'd lived the past three decades with my family at cancer's table, and now it was time to set a place for my husband. In a sense both macabre and fateful I felt I had been trained my whole life for this, to be standing in the face of death saying, "I know you well."

It was here I was given a choice: move forward with anger in all its familiarity, or tread in the unknown of hope and sorrow.

I had done anger before. She kept me alive when sadness would have swallowed me whole, stoking me forward when my broken heart wasn't ready to process the wholeness of my grief. While I didn't think I would survive anger a second time around, I was grateful for having been in her kiln. I now saw that she had made me who I was today—a woman shattered by grief, forged by fury, and strengthened to stand with all her broken pieces, a resounding renegade of grief.

With my sister by my side, I chose to leave anger in the background, always there but now just smoke in the harrowing blaze of sorrowful acceptance. There was no nobility in this decision, as I'd come to learn that both anger and sadness were equally important in the furnace of bereavement. In grief, everything we do is exactly what we have to do to survive.

Now was just my time to choose another path.

I had spent a lifetime cursing my rage. I'd buried myself in the search for better, the search for peace, the search for perfect, the search for power. I'd traveled the world hoping to find these things on a beach or in a pill or in a man, in my children's embrace, in a crowded club with a bottle in my hands or on my knees in prayer, desperate for forgiveness.

As a mother, I had come to believe that my quest for strength had been a series of dead-end mistakes. I was racked with shame thinking that my recklessness had led me down a path of self-destruction. But the truth was that every friendship, every lover, every rage-fueled tear, every new home, every runaway had been a roadmap. Every questionable decision I made had forged the path towards my own power. Even my father's death had been a steppingstone to myself.

My response to grief had not been breaking me.

It was building me.

Pain had laid the framework for empathy. Recklessness was the foundation to wisdom. Breaking was the joist of understanding that we rarely grow without first falling apart.

My brokenness was holding me together—a bridge through the gray I was learning to accept in all of its irreconciliation. My anger was the blueprint of a broken soul waiting to love herself in pieces, all at once.

My strength needed to be built before it could be found. And here I was, finding it exactly when I needed it.

"We're going to get him out of there, Ray. We're going to get him to an ECMO bed."

Rachel nodded and the world began moving forward once more. I ran to the basement with a layer of red mud caked to my sandals, sticky and thick from nights of heavy rain. I didn't even stop to scrape it off in the doorway, though I knew Rivs would be shaking his head at the copper footprints trailing across the floor he'd laid by hand.

I sat on Rivs's mattress with a pen and paper and asked Rachel to parse out transfer logistics with Dr. Avril while I made an online plea for ECMO resources. Throughout the past week, after Rivs's pre-sedation videos went viral on Instagram, thousands of people from across the globe had stepped forward to help our family, offering everything from medical resources to financial assistance and gifts for our children. At the time I had been too overwhelmed to accept their generous offers, feeling guilty for such momentous support when so many people were suffering at the hands of COVID-19 with little assistance. But when the one you love is fighting for life, ethical codes are blighted by the will to live.

When death comes to your home, you rage.

Within an hour of my post on social media, I had an inbox full of messages with ECMO resources from facilities across the continent.

I pored through the offerings, held by love in an intrinsically lonely time. In the midst of tragedy, I felt the heart of humanity.

Later I would wonder if that's what they had been trying to say in church all those years ago, in submitting to god. Maybe everyone was simply trying to crack themselves open to the ubiquity of love, knowing that we feel it best in the humbling narrows of pain. Maybe the message had been lost in translation over the years, over generations and transfers of power.

Maybe god was not found alone on our knees in submission but rather upright in pain, shoulder to shoulder as conduits of love, together in the terrible beauty of human experience.

Perhaps god was found in the confluence of love and pain.

And I was held in this convergence as I created a list of potential ECMO facilities. It was only moments later that Rachel tapped me on the shoulder looking defeated once again.

"Steph, Dr. Avril said they *could* transfer Rivs to a different hospital, but she thinks it will be impossible to find a team willing to accept him in his condition."

I had been preparing for these words but hearing them aloud was different.

"She said cancer is a strict disqualifier from ECMO, let alone for a newly diagnosed terminal lung cancer patient. To her knowledge, administering ECMO and chemo to a newly diagnosed stage IV lung cancer patient has never been done."

I nodded as she continued.

"Before transfer, we would need to find a cardiac surgeon, a pulmonologist, an intensivist, and an oncologist at the same hospital all on board to take his case. Dr. Avril said it would be highly unlikely if not impossible to find a team willing to receive him with his terminal diagnosis."

I understood the logic of her words, but something was telling me to keep pushing.

"I just want him to wake up, Ray. I want him to see how much the world loves him—how much *I* love him. If we only get a few hours together, that would be enough. I just need to give him the chance to feel it."

"Feel what?"

"The love," I said, and at once she understood.

Less than an hour later I received a call from Rivs's brother saying he'd found a physician in Phoenix willing to coordinate Rivs's transfer. The physician's name was Craig, a young ER doctor and avid distance runner who had recently stepped away from his medical practice to become a hospital transfer director after his own lymphoma diagnosis. While randomly scrolling through Instagram that afternoon, he saw my online plea and reached out.

"To be honest I'm not quite sure how this fell into place so quickly, but we've secured an ECMO bed in Scottsdale along with an entire medical team ready to take a chance on your husband," Craig said after I called him in shaking desperation. I could feel the critical passing of every minute Rivs lay in Flagstaff hospital.

"Thank you isn't enough, Craig. But thank you."

I scribbled the Scottsdale hospital's address along with names of the accepting physicians, each one a love letter to the universe.

> Dr. Riley—Directing Cardiac Surgeon
> Dr. Piercecchi—Accepting Cardiac Surgeon
> Dr. Assar—ICU Pulmonologist
> Dr. Briggs—Oncologist
> Dr. Fauble—Oncologist

"Don't thank me, Steph. I'm just proffering a chance. I've followed Rivs's athletic career since long before he got sick. He's inspired me in so many ways, from his grittiness in running to his gentle philosophy on life. I really think that if anyone can do this, it's him."

After we hung up, I wept. I had never felt so much pain, and I had never felt so much love. It felt like we had legions behind us, a battalion of warriors armed only with love and willing to fight on our behalf.

What a weapon.

What a miracle.

Craig was the first doctor to offer a shred of hope for Rivs's life in the past week, removed as he was from the details of his case. I wondered whether Craig's own confrontation with mortality had cracked him open—him being the intercessor of universal love, all of it flowing through him to me in that moment.

I walked to the fridge and opened a beer as Rachel made the necessary plans for Rivs's helicopter transfer to HonorHealth Scottsdale, which was scheduled for later that evening.

I left the basement as the sun hovered low in the sky, its meeting with the horizon a timekeeper for Rivs's departure and all the hours he would have to fight for breath on a ventilator. Julie was walking through our front door as I climbed the stairs—Harper, Iris, and Poppy following close behind with Mum heading up the rear, each of them wearing a tentative smile. I knew all too well how the twilight of a sick father shrouds the brilliance of things that normally bring joy. I held my daughters close, recognizing the guilt of that feeling. With redemptive awareness I also recognized that if I had survived grief, somehow, they would too—this knowing another binary gift of tragedy.

"Can I talk to you about transferring Tommy?" I asked Julie as she helped Poppy remove her shoes, perfectly dusted with sandstone from their hike. I needed Julie to understand the possibility that Rivs might not survive the hundred-and-fifty-mile flight to Scottsdale.

"He'll always be my boy, but he's your boy now, Steph. I support whatever you think is best." Julie cried in my arms as I laid out the plan, a tiny pair of shoes still gripped in her hand.

The rest of Rivs's family gave a similar response when I rushed a conference call to his father, grandmother, and five siblings between a few forced forkfuls of food. I'd had little appetite over the past several weeks, realizing how much weight I'd lost only when I changed my days-worn sweatpants for a pair of jean shorts in preparation for the sweltering Phoenix heat. When Mum saw the shorts hanging from my frame, she handed me a plate of roast chicken and mashed potatoes someone had dropped on our doorstep earlier that afternoon.

"Please eat, Steph," she said, her face worn with the same knowing I had for my own children, and in recognizing it so acutely, I ate.

For the first time in weeks, my hope had a path. I finished what little my stomach could hold before running into my bedroom to pack, unsure whether my stay in Phoenix would last a few days or a few weeks but unwilling to entertain the question as I jammed fistfuls of clothes into a backpack.

Two hours after my phone call with Craig, Rachel and I left for Phoenix with Harper and Rachel's daughter Summer, while Mum and Julie stayed home in Flagstaff with Poppy and Iris. They said they would wait at home for a few days to "see how things unfolded"—a euphemism for the death-dealing question it seemed none of us wanted to answer.

The moonless sky burned with lightning as we drove towards the valley, the thunder a roiling percussion leading us along. I watched the passing scenery shift from high-altitude forest to scaly mesquite before a desert of saguaros while Harper and Summer giggled together in the back seat.

"How quickly everything changes," I thought, contemplating the necessity of compartmentalization in tragedy—about the Mad Libs I'd played with Phil the night Dad died, about the guilt I'd felt for laughing when Dad's body lay in the next room, about how happy I was to hear Harper laugh amidst the sadness, all of it shifting, all of it engulfed in the topography of impermanence. I thought about how keeping my grief in a box had helped me survive until I had been ready to feel it.

"Please don't feel guilty," I wanted to say to Harper or to the fourteen-year-old me. Continuing to live is how we survive a confrontation with death. There is no merit in wading through the pain. When crossing the badlands of grief, release is sometimes the only way through.

There is no shame in it.

The storm finally erupted as Rachel pulled into our Scottsdale hotel. A torrential downpour flooded the streets as Guardian Air called to inform me that the transport team was unable to fly Rivs through the lightning.

"We'll have to wait for the skies to clear before moving your husband. If the weather continues as forecast, we should have him packaged for flight by 9 a.m. tomorrow."

I ended the call after giving verbal consent for transport, the word "packaged" lingering in my mind as I imagined Rivs's body hooked to machines, bundled in off-white sheets and flying through angry clouds, packed on a gurney like freight. I trusted the flight team would be respectful, but the image still made me shudder. I tried not to count the extra hours Rivs would be left struggling on the ventilator as I fell asleep next to Rachel while Summer and Harper whispered together far past bedtime, wrapped in the pithiness of youth.

The next morning, Rivs was flown safely to the Scottsdale hospital, even after a phone call from his night nurse, who informed me that she didn't think he would be deemed stable enough for transport.

"His blood pressure and oxygen sats are low and his heart rate is high. He's on pressor medication and 100 percent vent oxygen. I just want to prepare you for the possibility that the flight crew might not accept your husband for transport," she said early the next morning as I sat by the hotel pool with Rachel, giving in to the sun as Harper and Summer dived for the coins we'd tossed.

At the time I had resented that nurse, along with Dr. Avril and Dr. Hemmerman, the critical care doctor who seemed somewhat indifferent to Rivs's condition the day I had visited him.

Looking back I would see that they were all executing their jobs as directed, endowed with the unimaginable task of discerning statistics of life and death amid exception, recognizing that COVID-19 only made that job even more impossible. It just so happened that Rivs *was* an exception, one who couldn't be lobbied for in most cases. By definition, Rivs was panning out to be a medical miracle.

Though I had fought against the term my entire adult life, I was beginning to see that miracles weren't reserved for the sick or the living. In their true form they encompass life, death, the resounding thereof, and all the spaces between.

I believe my father understood this porous truth as he left his own life with a patient knowing; sometimes, it takes generations to see the miracle.

* * *

On July 23, 2020, at 9 a.m., three weeks after his initial admission to the Flagstaff hospital, Rivs was received at HonorHealth Scottsdale. Within a few hours of his admission, I received individual calls from both the receiving ICU Pulmonologist, Dr. Assar, as well as Dr. Piercecchi, the cardiac surgeon who would put Rivs on ECMO later that day.

"He's living hour to hour right now—maybe even minute to minute—but I promise I'm going to try my best to save him," Dr. Assar said, the confidence in his voice calming my nerves. "Your husband's running career has been a huge inspiration for me to get back into shape over the past couple years. My hope is that I'll be sharing a few miles with him sometime in the future."

"It's a long shot, but I have hope," Dr. Piercecchi later offered in his calm, matter-of-fact way, his voice both cool and commanding as I clutched the phone to my ear. "Medicine is more art than science, and for a case like Rivs's, it's going to take harmony between a multitude of different specialties. Harmony and, well, some plain luck. People see doctors as infallible, but the truth is that sometimes we get it right, and sometimes we don't. I can't promise you he's going to make it, but I *can* promise that we're going to work together to try our best. Remember, this is a marathon, not a sprint. And I think you might understand that concept better than anyone."

The next day was a whirlwind of phone calls of varying consent for

Rivs's body, including ECMO surgery, a tracheostomy for long-term ventilation, bronchoscopies to suction out necrotic lung tissue, and a pericardial window surgery to remove excess fluid from around his heart. He also started on an aggressive chemotherapy regimen known as SMILE, an acronym for steroid (dexamethasone), methotrexate, ifosfamide, L-asparaginase, and etoposide—the most ironically named cancer treatment I could think of.

NK/T-cell lymphoma was an extremely rare and aggressive cancer that was notoriously difficult to diagnose. The five-year prognosis for this type of cancer was grim, and as far as we knew, fewer than ten people had been diagnosed with Rivs's particular primary lung manifestation in medical history. Grimmer still was the fact that none of these ten patients had survived. Due to the unique circumstance of starting a terminal lung cancer patient on both chemo and ECMO, his oncologists decided to omit L-asparaginase from his treatment protocol, predicting that this highly toxic chemotherapy would kill Rivs before the cancer got around to it. This was a precarious omission because L-asparaginase was proven to be the most promising medication for fighting NK/T-cell lymphoma. The oncologists also decided to cut his methotrexate dosage in half to reduce the risk of tumor lysis syndrome, which is a systemic diffusion of toxic buildup from dying tumors. The doctors openly admitted that no one knew if this tightrope walk between over and under medication would work. Everyone was simply hoping that his survival would be found somewhere in the balance.

Later that evening I received another call—this time from the Flagstaff oncologist who had been assigned to Rivs's case in the sixteen hours between his diagnosis and transfer.

"I want you to know how relieved I am that you got him out of here. We don't have the resources to treat your husband in Flagstaff. I'm really glad you pushed for ECMO. Whatever happens, I want you to know that you did the right thing."

I thanked him, his words a loving hand reached across the void of second guesses and responsibility, fear and guilt.

You did the right thing. For once, I had trusted myself.

* * *

The next day, Dr. Assar and Dr. Piercecchi pulled the necessary strings to allow me to visit the ICU.

Rachel and I were floating on inflatable unicorns in an Airbnb pool under the blazing Phoenix sun when my phone rang to deliver the news. It was another gleaming display of privilege I accepted eagerly, though tainted by guilt knowing how many people were dying alone in hospital beds across the globe, their families clamoring for comfort on pixelated video calls. Still, I was elated to be brought forth from the purgatory of waiting somewhere far away to the opportunity to be right by Rivs's side. I said the words aloud to Rachel.

"I'm going to visit my husband. He is dying on a ventilator in the ICU."

Rachel's eyes brimmed with tears. I placed my phone on the pool deck and paddled towards her. She extended her hand and I held it.

"My husband has . . . fucking lung cancer," I said in a sob before falling into laughter.

"Lung cancer!" Rachel cackled, and we laughed until our sides hurt, two fatherless daughters floating together in tragedy once again, shoulder to shoulder in the beauty and terror of life.

CHAPTER 16

Time is round.

It isn't linear like I once believed. It folds in on itself, like grief or a father's face when he tells his children he's dying, like a lung or two sisters drifting around death over and over again.

Time twists around, tethered by memory. It collapses, then circles back to teach us things we missed the first time—lessons that are sometimes only visible through the rawness of pain. In the totality of heartbreak I was beginning to recognize time's pliability, understanding life itself as an elemental cycle of trial and error.

We're born, we try, we learn, we change, we die, we're born again once more, all in one lifetime.

And sometimes, all at once.

The afternoon of my poolside conversation with Dr. Assar, I prepared myself to see Rivs in the Scottsdale hospital. I brushed my hair and pulled on the faded gray T-shirt he loved me wearing. I stood in the hospital's COVID-19 screening line, then walked down the ICU hallways, trying to remember the directions to his room.

Did they say left or right at the NICU? What if he dies while I'm there? Did they tell me to pass the telemetry unit? Oh god did I wear the right shirt?

As I approached the ICU, I was met by a smiling nurse who wrapped a hazmat-suited arm around my shoulder and led me through the department's mechanical doors. I took a deep breath when we stopped in front of his room, preparing myself for what I might find on the other side of the door. Would I feel the same sense of calm I had experienced while next to him at the Flagstaff hospital?

The year before, Rivs and I traveled to Japan for one of his work trips. Beyond the stunning landscapes and organized cities, what made the deepest visual impression on us was the many toriis found throughout the country, humble wooden arches built at the entrances of Shinto shrines that acted as physical markers between the mundane and the sacred. We'd see these toriis everywhere from Nagano to Tokyo, peppered among quiet forests and dotted throughout bustling cities, all of them modest and understated, each one of them offering a truth everyone seemed to revere if not believe: *beyond here lies the sacred*. Though I didn't believe in a spiritual realm, I was touched by the symbolism: amid the chaos of life, take a moment to bow to the things we cannot see.

Now, as I stood in the doorway to Rivs's room, I felt I was standing at my own torii, that I was quite literally passing from mundane to sacred as I walked towards him. As I stepped into the domain of the in-between that was his new room—big and bright and teeming with productive energy—it became clear to me that calm wasn't a *feeling*. It was a choice.

Looking over his body that was now hooked to an ECMO circuit with a ventilator running through a tracheotomy in his neck, I knew that I was no longer in the land of the living. But I wasn't in the domain of the dying, either. This was a holy space—dark and light, liminal and full, devoid of rules and definition.

Here, I was not a victim of trauma. Here I would *choose* calm.

When everything else was outside of my control, I was still in charge of my emotions—even if being in charge meant falling apart.

Would I focus on the bloody chemo sores in Rivs's mouth, or would I see how comfortable he looked now that the ventilator was run through the tracheostomy in his neck rather than down his throat? Would I hover in the anger of reliving a childhood trauma or be grateful for the perspective I had earned from living something similar once before?

I was heartbroken to see Rivs hooked to so many machines and lines, but there was also peace in it. Peace amidst the chaos.

I was beginning to see that the way in which I approached life—the narratives I wrote about my position in the world and the stories I told about myself and others—informed meaning itself. It was how I defined difficult situations that influenced the emotional outcome of a given circumstance. In suffering I could own the meaning of my pain—all of it subjective, all of it personal to the meaning I ascribed through those choices.

And in owning the meaning, I could make it, too.

* * *

After that first visit, I was granted full visitation right on the grounds that Rivs did not have COVID-19 and was likely at the end of his life.

As the days continued, Rivs's room became a sanctuary—a vermilion cliff between worlds. With corner windows that looked out onto a gray hospital catwalk and the constant shuffling of feet convening around his bed, his room was a vacuum where all worldly distractions were sucked away. It was a conduit, a gateway to holy things I knew I could never put into words, but here we were, together in the indelible now, stark and stunning.

Nothing existed on either side of each moment. Nothing else mattered but here. It was heaven and hell all at once.

There was a purity to that time, like I was being reintroduced to the space between life and death with which I would quickly grow reacquainted—a space I'd soon learn was just as real as the poles on either side of it. Rather than feel helpless and lost by his bedside, I felt empowerment, peace, and love.

I held his hand and whispered words that transformed the mundane to sacred—the sound of Poppy's nighttime singing, the colors of Iris's butterfly painting, the grass stains on Harper's knees from catching another lizard. As monitors beeped a set of dangerous vital signs I knew that nothing about living had ever been mundane. These things had always been sacred.

What a gift to love and be loved.

I had never felt so alive as I lived each divinely human moment alongside him. Each breath was something beautiful, and every breath had always been miraculous.

Sometimes I would speak to him out loud, whispering in rushed sentences whenever both his nurse and respiratory therapist were out of the room, which was seldom. Rivs's condition was so critical that he required two-on-one medical attention at all times, barring the medical staff's quick bathroom breaks. During those few minutes of solitude I threw out memories like maybe they were lifelines.

Remember when I bleached my hair and it turned out looking like Justin Timberlake's curly mop in the late '90s? How later that day you knelt beside me in the bathroom and shaved my head while platinum hair fluttered around us like straw? Remember how you told me I was the most beautiful thing you'd ever seen right there on the bathroom floor as you smoothed your hands over my scalp?

Remember when Iris used to eat cat food like it was her favorite snack? How eventually we gave up trying to stop her and let her eat it by the handful?

Remember the first time we surfed together? The sunscreen bled into my eyes after the first set rolled through and I thought I was blind. I paddled around screaming for you as the waves rocked me, over and over. In the end we both couldn't help but laugh when you finally found me, my eyes squeezed shut while my hands searched for you, frantic.

Rivs? Rivs? Are you there? Where are you, Rivs?

Remember, remember, remember.

Usually I'd reach for him in other ways, with my hand over his and my forehead leaned towards his face, yearning for proximity. I could feel Rivs best when I was close to him. I was beginning to wonder whether it was his spirit I was feeling, and if so, was my dad's spirit somewhere close as well?

I was terrified, yes. But I was with him. And somehow that was enough. Somehow it *is* enough when you realize that everything that ever happens is found in a single inhale, that all of life exists inside each and every moment.

What is more alive than a declaration of presence on the precipice of death? Being *here, now*, the feeling is more human, more perfect, more divine than any drug, any god, any man.

* * *

As predicted, Rivs's body began to break down soon after starting chemotherapy, once the neon-yellow liquid dripping into his veins had accumulated in his sedated body to wreak havoc on his organs. Due to the unknowns of starting chemotherapy while on ECMO—a device that inherently destroys red blood cells—the doctors needed to find a balance between slowing Rivs's cancer growth while keeping his body strong enough to withstand life support.

Essentially, they needed to kill Rivs just enough to keep him alive.

"Rivs's liver is beginning to fail," his oncologist, Dr. Briggs, said as we stood in the hallway outside his room. It was day four of chemo, time now marked by the administration of chemicals, the entire universe a twenty-one-day calendar: five days of chemotherapy followed by sixteen days of recovery cycling over and over until remission or death.

"He's too unstable to get a CT scan, but we assume that the cancer has spread to his liver, as well as to his spleen. I'm sorry," she said, her choppy bangs hanging over the top of her face shield as she spoke with curtness and sympathy—traits likely bred from years in dealing with dire prognoses and the obstinate chasm between sickness and health. Still, I could feel a softness seeping through her yellow PPE gown, inured only by the directness of her words.

I loved her for both.

I nodded my head, trying to remain calm as we stood together in the hall between the ICU and the bone marrow transplant unit, where Rivs would eventually be transferred if he survived. I looked around. The space between those two doors was an endless gulf between life and death. Their physical proximity mocked the journey we'd have to endure in order to travel from one to another, the hallway separating them a cruel delineation.

So *lonely*.

The next day, on July 28, at 8 a.m., Rivs started to crash. I had just made the short drive from our Airbnb to the hospital after forcing myself to swallow a few bites of buttered toast Mum had shoved in my hand on my way out. I greeted the hospital reception workers before taking the elevator to the second floor. I made my way towards the ICU, waving to the security guard who now smiled at me sympathetically instead of asking for my credentials.

As I followed the silent hallways I remembered a conversation I'd had with my mum years earlier, when Harper had turned three—the age Phil had been when he was diagnosed with leukemia. Overcome with empathy once I had a child that same age, I asked how she had endured the trauma of his cancer treatment. Mum simply shrugged her shoulders and said, "You just do it." I remember thinking it had been a deflective response, but it was precisely how I felt now while walking into the unimaginable that had become my reality—a sense of existential unfolding. There was nothing noble about the way I approached Rivs's sickness. I just did it. Often, what looks like resilience to others is simply accepting the things we can't change.

I walked through the ICU doors, expecting to be greeted by Sarah, the lead respiratory therapist in charge of Rivs's ECMO circuit, who was now a close friend. But this morning, as with the outcome of almost any expectation—the harbinger of all disappointment—I entered his room to see the entire medical staff circling around Rivs's bed in observation, his shallow breaths jerking his body as the numbers on his oxygen monitor plummeted.

88.

86.

84.

82.

The alarms wailed, and the medical staff spoke in hushed urgency, and I stood there, frozen.

Rivs was in both respiratory and liver failure. The metabolic demand of processing chemo was further affecting his compromised ability to exchange oxygen and carbon dioxide—a mechanism already burdened by a massive lung tumor load. He was drowning on dry land despite two life support machines. The interstitial fluid in his lungs had accumulated to suffocating levels. Once again, they were collapsing.

I stood alone on the outskirts of the medical circle, watching. Dr. Piercecchi was involved in a conversation with the perfusionist. Dr. Assar was prepping for a bronchoscopy to remove excess fluid from Rivs's lungs. His nurse Anna was busy administering a paralytic, hoping that physical catatonia might ease his struggling breath. Sarah was altering the settings on his ventilator, trying to find a mechanical solution for his failing respiratory system.

For the first time in Rivs's presence since his illness, I cried.

I was terrified. I was devastated. And I was fucking angry. Today there was no choice.

"*This is it,*" I thought. "*The betrayal of hope.*"

I had been expecting it all along, but it felt different this time. The landing was a little softer, somehow. Less unexpected, perhaps. I was thinking these things when a warm hand caressed the small of my back.

I open my eyes and turn to see a woman from the housekeeping staff holding a tissue with a cracked and calloused hand.

"Here. You take, my love."

I've seen her almost every day since visiting Rivs. I've watched her mop the floor and linger around his bed in seeming reverence. I've picked up my feet and thanked her sheepishly as she cleans the floor around me, as one does when they feel the shameful weight of their privilege. I've watched her eye my husband's sedated body, whispering under her breath words I can't make out. She appears to be in her late sixties and by the way she greets me in accented English whenever I pull my chair next to his bed, I assume she is from somewhere in Eastern Europe. Now I realize that I don't know her name.

I accept the tissue and dry my eyes as she wraps an arm around my waist.

"Thanks god, my dear, I pray for you. I pray every day for you and him," she says, motioning the sign of the cross before resting her head on my shoulder.

I lean into her and for a little while we stand together in silence, floating in the universal experience of sorrow, forever bonded by a simple and momentous act of love.

Time folds in on itself.

Despite the immediacy of life slipping away and the pragmatic hands working to keep it, once again I am anchored by a stranger's love.

"I'm Steph," I say.

"Fringa." She glances up, her eyes a deep well of knowing, cracked on the edges in a way that makes her look perpetually caught between tears and a smile.

After a few moments or maybe forever, she turns from me.

"I go now, my dear." She reaches for her mop bucket and hurries out the door before I have time to thank her. I watch her walk down the ICU hallway, her back bent forward as she pulls the weight of the bucket behind her, her gray hair frizzing out around her ears.

After Fringa left, I looked around the room to see the same scene—the bleach-washed floors, the salmon pink walls decorated with photos and cards I had brought from home, the lines and tubes snaking in and out of Rivs's body, the medical team huddled around his bed in calculated chaos. The scene was the same, but something had shifted, Fringa's gesture of love having softened the sharpness of my nerves and aching doubt, changing the meaning of it all.

I was still terrified by Rivs's deteriorating condition but somehow, I didn't feel so lonely. Yes, I was still scared and devastated and angry. Yes, he was still struggling and swollen and drowning. And though the circumstance hadn't changed, something inside me had, as it had been slowly doing over the past few weeks. Or perhaps it was less a change and more an emergence, an awakening of that which had always been inside me. An excavation. For the first time since his illness, I knew that no matter the outcome, *I* was going to be okay. I could now see the love that had always been waiting around me. Finally, I had somewhere to put it.

Here.

I looked at Rivs's body once again, grounding myself as I was grounded by Fringa, feeling a transformative power fill the room. As I stood in the nakedness of now, in the undeniable space that is both spinning and inert, it was clear that life is fluid and always shifting, always moving, and still always anchored by love.

I allowed myself to feel it all: the fear, the anger, the sorrow, the subtle beauty leaking in through the cracks, the everythingness of pain, and the love wrapped around it soft and loud and invisible—all of it intrinsically connected, each moment a shared experience. In confronting Rivs's mortality I was learning how to love. I was learning how to be sad. I was understanding life as magnificently tragic and love as omnipresent, both of them occurring always, right now.

Maybe there *was* room for all of it. Maybe there was room for all of me. Maybe I didn't have to choose.

Though I had waged war against myself and the world to define love in finite ways, I was beginning to see that it had always been infinite, woven into every experience of my life without rules, without judgment.

It was beyond me and within me—inside pain and joy simultaneously. Throughout my life, despite what I'd been taught as a child, everything denoted that love was the experience of everything other than perfection. Love lived in gray, above and below stereotypes, outside of dogma and rules, around betterness and between black and white.

Love was the antithesis to *perfect*.

Perfection was simply loving myself while broken, to move forward while human. To strive for nothing but accepting exactly where I was at.

To simply be here, now.

Within an hour of my exchange with Fringa, Rivs's oxygen came back up after Sarah switched his ventilator to APRV mode, overriding his natural breath and forcing his lungs to comply with the mechanical respiration he was still fighting against. For now, at least, he was stable.

I left the hospital later that day with an assurance from Dr. Piercecchi that he would do everything within his control to make Rivs comfortable. I wanted to be close to him, but I knew there was little I could do in such a medically acute situation. I drove away from the hospital acknowledging that sometimes owning our power means deferring to others when things are outside of our control. Sometimes strength is found in surrender.

That evening I went home and poured myself a pint of wine—one of the coping mechanisms I'd leaned on throughout Rivs's sickness and one I wouldn't have changed in retrospect because it allowed me to escape the trauma of each day. I snuggled in bed next to my girls, grateful they had stayed awake long enough to listen to my lullabies, my voice quivering.

Dr. Piercecchi called later that night to say they had started Rivs on Lasix, a diuretic drip to flush out the excess fluid accumulating in his lungs, as well as repositioned the ECMO catheter in his heart, giving him an increase of oxygenated blood flow. The infectious disease physician had also found two strains of fungal infections in his blood, which rendered him septic and further burdened his ability to transport oxygen throughout his body. They had started him on an aggressive antifungal that would hopefully kill the infection before it killed him.

I went to bed terrified but comforted by knowing that Rivs was being cared for with an attentiveness I'd never imagined in the medical world. Dr. Piercecchi was invested far beyond the call of duty, visiting the hospital on his off days and working around the clock to ensure Rivs had the highest chance of survival. It wasn't unusual for me to get an update text from Piercecchi at four in the morning—hours before his scheduled shift. Dr. Assar had made a habit of calling the night nurse to make sure Rivs was meticulously tended to when the day staff was away, checking his labs and scans even while on vacation. Dr. Briggs and Dr. Fauble were actively researching cutting-edge NK/T-cell lymphoma treatments and conferring with specialists from around the country, having never before treated a patient with Rivs's specific cancer.

Yes, it was their job. But it felt a lot like love.

That night I laid in bed reflecting on Fringa's kindness—how it had anchored me, how it felt to be held by a stranger when everything was falling apart. I marveled at the strength that came from it, understanding how necessary it is for pain to be grounded by love in order to be fully realized, recognizing them as two flickers of the same flame.

Love and pain.

Hope and fear.

Power and surrender.

Not vestiges of black and white but bridges between the gray. It was within—in accepting the breadth between them—that truth was found.

Here was peace. *Here* was power. *Here* was better. *Here* was love.

Fringa was the intercessor for it that day, but I had been the recipient of immeasurable love and kindness throughout Rivs's hospitalization. It had been pouring in from across the globe in supportive messages on social media, from our Flagstaff community who'd organized fundraisers for our family, and from friends offering to help in any way they could. It had come through in a practical sense when a GoFundMe created by a group of Rivs's friends began to accumulate a staggering sum of donation money, which allowed me to focus on our family and devote my energy to keeping Rivs alive rather than worry about living expenses, medical bills, and the unavoidable question of how we would survive financially if he died.

Though most of this love was coming from people I had never met, it felt deeply meaningful. In fact, it meant everything to know that I wasn't alone. I often felt unworthy of the help I was receiving, guilty with the heaviness from being the recipient of a generosity I knew I could never repay. Why was I receiving so much support when others had so little? But here it was, all around me: love, support, help, encouragement. All I could do was accept it, to move past dangerous thoughts that erroneously denoted love as a terminable resource.

It was the purest expression of humanity—love for no other reason than love itself. Altruism in its purest sense. It was something I had been offered throughout my life: the kind policeman in Montreal, Bishop Huang, Marc, my twilight car ride in Honduras, Solomon. Even in the depths of self-loathing I had been able to accept these offerings, not knowing that through their love I would one day find my own.

For the first time I was hearing myself through other people's words, seeing myself through other people's eyes, and allowing myself to accept the love that had always existed, even when I couldn't find it in myself.

After years of searching for validation, I was finally seeing a reflection of what had been inside me all along. I was learning that love was unending, looping and cyclical, permeable and porous—an innately renewable resource. The more I allowed, the more I received, and the more I could give.

Love is light—only fully realized when it is reflected.

It was never meant to be kept.

And now when I think of god, I see Fringa in forest green scrubs.

CHAPTER 17

It was just before 6 a.m. on July 31, one week after Rivs started chemo and fifteen days from when he was first sedated, that I was awakened by the metallic ping of a text message receipt. The sun had just started peeking through white linen curtains, casting a golden glow over a bed that was not my own. Despite my objection, Mum and Julie had insisted that I take the master bedroom of our Phoenix rental house. While I appreciated their offer, sleeping in it somehow made me feel lonelier, inhabiting a sprawling space without anyone to share it with.

Jolted by the sound, I fumbled for my phone to see a message from Dr. Piercecchi.

"Rivs is awake! Come in ASAP."

I rolled out of bed, my eyes still heavy with sleep as I threw a bra on under my shirt and slipped on the same pair of denim shorts I'd been living in for the past three weeks.

Aware that Rivs's conscious ability to fight was crucial to his survival, that morning Dr. Piercecchi decided to turn off his sedating medications for an hour-long "sedation vacation." I later learned that this was a daily practice for most sedated patients, but Rivs's condition had been so critical that any change to his treatment or medication would have been catastrophic. Even a slight shift of his body would cause his oxygen to plummet, necessitating the "do not move" protocol that eventually led to a bone-deep bedsore on his sacrum from constant pressure. Now, though Rivs's medical circumstance hadn't changed, the need for his conscious cooperation outweighed the risk of waking him up.

The hallmark characteristics of Rivs's personality—grit and determination—were now integral to the battle for his life.

I scribbled a note to Mum and Julie—I LEFT EARLY. RIVS IS AWAKE! LOVE YOU ALL XOXO—before jumping in my car. I always liked to be home when the girls woke up, to enjoy my coffee while sitting with them for breakfast and talking about Rivs's milestones or setbacks as tenderly as I could. But today I couldn't leave the house soon enough. Each passing minute was a predator of time.

I drove to the hospital in a daze, my mind ablaze with expectation as I imagined how Rivs's eyes would meet my own when I walked into his room—how he'd radiate recognition and the two of us would be reunited in a fairy tale of triumph and survival. In tragic innocence I imagined these things all the way up until I walked into his room, where I was met by jaundiced eyes that opened into slits staring across the room, blankly, into nothingness.

I walked towards him and waved to Anna, Rivs's nurse, who was standing by his bed in anticipation. I couldn't understand why she looked so eager. To me he looked uncomfortable and lifeless—farther away than I'd ever seen him. He was a shell of a human with no shred of recognition behind his empty stare, a far cry from the man I knew in life and nowhere near the presence I'd felt in the space between here and death.

Now was the first time I saw my father in Rivs's face, the diuretics having drained his edema, exposing all that had been eaten away by cancer and weeks of immobility. But mostly it was his eyes that re-minded me of Dad—the vacancy to them, the vastness that spoke of the distance between the men they once were and that which lay before me.

So lonely.

I was angry that no one told me what "waking up" would look like, even when I knew that nothing could have prepared me for it. When readying to greet a loved one while meeting and mourning them at the same time, words just fall short. I knew this even then. And still, standing in front of Rivs I was overcome with the kind of disappointment that is only found at the end of expectation.

Weren't you just right here?

I stood frozen at the foot of his bed. Anna linked her arm loosely through mine with as much affection as COVID-19 regulations would allow before returning to her computer in the corner of his room. Oh, how I loved her. She was an incredible nurse who brought me homemade cookies on her shifts and always took extra care to make Rivs comfortable. Most mornings I would come into his room to find her gently scrubbing his scalp or massaging his feet with oils she'd brought from home, talking to him like an old friend while he lay there, motionless.

Calmed by her love I walked closer to him, past Paul, his respiratory therapist, who was sitting beside the ECMO circuit registering hourly blood stats. Paul was bald and slightly overweight and always had something snippy to say about the news that played as background noise in Rivs's room. He nodded with encouragement as I shimmied by him, the space in the room overtaken by machines and lines.

"Eyes off the monitor," he warned, knowing by now my propensity to watch Rivs's vital signs. "Your eyes aren't going to change anything, sweetheart. Just be here."

I nodded and sat in my chair, trying to subdue the disappointment. It was the first time I realized just how sick Rivs was, just how weak, just how unlike him. It affected me more than almost anything had so far in his illness. I knew I had a choice to see the good, but right then it all just fucking sucked. It was all terror and no beauty and all I could do was be in it, eyes off the monitor, mired in the humanness of the moment.

"It's not supposed to be like this," I thought, brutally aware that nothing is ever the way it's supposed to be. And still I tried to pull the pieces back together, to marry expectation with trauma in a union doomed from the start.

I reached for his withered hand, ran my fingers over his, and held on to them a little more tentatively than usual. Touching a hand both familiar and foreign was achingly reminiscent. I tried not to shudder as his eyes maintained their vapid stare.

"Hey, babe." I leaned into him, trying to settle into a place that was neither life nor death nor the space between them—a place I didn't yet have words for, and maybe I never will.

"I love you, babe. I miss you."

I paused.

"Anyways, Harper is doing pretty well."

I was nervous and I was searching, groping for something that might stoke his desire to keep fighting as I wrapped my hand more firmly around his.

"She's been making these cute clay figurines. You'd love them. Poppy just discovered her love for ballet and insists on wearing her leotard and ballet shoes everywhere we go."

I tried to measure my words, to bridle my sorrow, to subdue the fear that muddied my thoughts, to curb the madness that comes with calculated time.

"Both our moms have been so good to them. They're always dancing and singing and going on adventures together. They know you're really sick but they're being spoiled with love and attention. Oh, I almost forgot to tell you—Iris lost her first tooth!"

I was rambling. Floundering. I was on a first date, not knowing what to say or how to present myself. I closed my eyes, silently begging for a relic of presence but there he remained.

Spiritless. Catatonic.

I bowed my head.

Please, Rivs. Please. Just let me know you're still here, I thought. Or had I prayed it?

I opened my eyes and studied his face, from his shedding eyelashes to his beard that had started falling out in thick patches. He was still so beautiful.

Please, Rivs. Please.

And then I watched as a single tear fell from the corner of his motionless eye.

I inhaled sharply.

"Babe, can you hear me?"

And then he smiled, short and brief. His eyes remained vacant but his mouth curled upward in a magnificent declaration of being. He had made his way through the cosmos. Tearing through the thick of it just to assure me that he was still here. Still fighting. Still resolved to live.

Him, comforting me.

It was the most devastating and exquisite thing I'd ever seen.

I hear you better here, too, I said, my head bent down on his chest, my lips unmoving.

Seconds later, Rivs's oxygen began to dip as his heart rate soared dangerously.

Anna walked to his IV station and reset his sedation drips.

Just like that, he floated away.

* * *

The subsequent three weeks brought a variety of setbacks, from internal bleeds to the need for more chest tubes to a handful of systemic infections. As Rivs continued to decline, Dr. Piercecchi decided to place an additional ECMO catheter in his femoral vein for extra oxygenated blood flow. During this procedure, Rivs's oxygen dropped into the 30s and his heart rate dipped to 20 beats per minute when an air bubble became trapped in the ECMO circuit. The medical team acted quickly—clamping the compromised circuit and replacing the ECMO machine within a matter of minutes.

The next day, Rivs's lead perfusionist, a kind-eyed man named Sam, explained why Rivs needed the additional catheter.

"We've never seen such a strong heart," he marveled as the new tube ran rich with reoxygenated blood. I could see it stitched to Rivs's leg, from mid-thigh to pelvis, his condition too critical for formalities like hospital gowns. I was now used to seeing him bare bodied on the hospital bed, his medical need for lines and catheters rendering any form of covering an encumbrance to his treatment. Most days I'd come in to see Rivs splayed out on the bed completely nude, sheathed only by a white hand towel.

"I'm both alarmed and impressed by his cardiac output," Sam continued, the kindness in his voice as comforting as his understated intelligence. "His heart pumps a massive volume of blood each minute, which requires extra blood volume to support his oxygen demand. This is a problem, but it's also the reason he's been able to withstand so much stress. I've never seen a heart rate consistently in the 130 beats per minute range for weeks without succumbing to a heart attack. Your husband's ability to pump blood and absorb oxygen at a cellular level is unprecedented. Honestly, I don't think anyone else could have survived this. I believe that extreme fitness is keeping your husband alive."

I nodded my head, my hands wringing around the cardigan sweater I'd started leaving in the ICU closet next to my water bottle and a small stack of books. I thanked Sam for his explanation, making sure to acknowledge the "Run with Rivs" logo he wore under his white medical coat, printed across one of the T-shirts Rivs's athletic sponsor had created as a fundraising campaign for our family. In the coming weeks, I'd see almost the entire ICU staff wearing something from the "Team Rivs" apparel line.

"Slow and steady deposits," I whispered in Rivs's ear after Sam left the room, restating the training mantra Rivs had repeated over the years as he conditioned his mind and body to endure extremes and weather the unfathomable.

"I want to be ready when the storm comes," he once said when I asked him to cut back on one of his weekend training runs. "It'll all be worth it someday."

* * *

One month before his fateful canyon run, Rivs comes home from a long run, raw from miles on his feet.

It isn't unusual for him to return from the mountains as exposed as the craggy trails he summits, his countenance sage like from hours of fatigue and glycogen depletion, as though the forest is its own house of meditation. During these communions, Rivs often finds clarity. Sometimes, he shares this clarity with me.

This afternoon he walks through the door and stumbles into my arms, sobbing.

"I don't have many days left, babe."

"What do you mean?"

"I don't know. I just saw it today when I was out in the woods. I'm running out of days. I don't know if it's weeks or years I have left. But, Steph—we don't grow old together. I saw it. I'm so sorry," he says, as though apologizing for another unfinished race.

I hold him and cry. I don't know what to say.

But now I understand; Rivs has always known what he was training for.

And maybe I have always known, too.

I hear you.

CHAPTER 18

And the days went on like this: Rivs's life hovering on the brink while he woke sporadically and sometimes not at all.

All the while love poured in from around the world, moving through the universe and finding its way to me. I knew I was absorbing and channeling this love to him whenever we were together. I knew it needed a human conduit to be transferred because I could feel it even as his body lay in sedation—a subtle but undeniable exchange that occurred whenever I placed my hands on his delicate skin.

This reciprocation was more a communion of spirit than an exchange of words.

It was a prayer.

After spending days together in the in-between, I learned that I could directly connect with Rivs while he slept rather than offer intercessory prayers to an interventionist god. It wasn't a sudden realization but a discovery that built slowly, quietly, in those sacred liminal spaces. The more time I spent with him, the better I could hear him. The better I could hear myself.

I had dismissed the concept of prayer after my own had failed to save my father in the ways I expected, but through Rivs's illness I started to redefine the practice. I started to see that prayers weren't self-righteous aspirations to be petitioned through a deified middleman but simply love offered up to the universe, words of intention released with hope, devoid of expectation.

Even when medical knowledge indicated otherwise, I was sure that Rivs was still *here*. Still fighting. Still resolved to live. It wasn't a transaction of words but a transfer of awareness. Though my rational side balked against this admission, I now knew our souls were speaking to each other. Words, time, space—these concepts had no authority here, where an eternity of love was expressed in the blink of an eye.

In the rawness of this very real place there was no need for an intermediary. Rivs was just as present here as he had been in the physical world. When I sat next to his sedated body, there was palpable energy. I could hear him through a wildness of spirit and the warmth burning in my chest. In confronting Rivs's death, I had never felt more alive.

I hear you.

The only way I was able to make sense of this was through my experience with psychedelics. I had once before traveled to an alternate time and space—an inter-dimensional place of bending realities and infinite love. Why couldn't I do it now, while my husband wrestled between them?

Even after the most difficult hospital days I'd laugh to Rachel that mushrooms were saving my life. Had I never experienced such transcendentalism at the behest of magic fungi, I might not have been open to the possibility of this line of communication.

"What a trip," I'd say to her on the phone while driving back to my Airbnb, and we'd laugh with the purgative irreverence that flows when someone you love is dead or slowly dying.

Why this collective energy of love could comfort some and not others, I still did not understand. Watching my little brother survive leukemia while his closest childhood friends passed away in the arms of devastated parents, it was impossible to believe in a fatalistic hierarchy of purpose. Having witnessed my father's death despite being surrounded by overwhelming love, the notion that love could selectively "save" some and not others was unfathomable. The idea that certain people had "more work to do" in this world was repulsive. The term "being called home to Heaven" made me irate. While I understood the intention behind these sentiments, I also recognized the audacity of suggesting that a mother's dead child might have more purpose in any place other than cradled in her arms, alive.

What felt true now was that perhaps love and prayer were simply channels to carry people through, a little more gently, towards whatever outcome lay before them. Like miracles, maybe healing rarely manifested how or when we expected it. Maybe it took decades or even generations to recognize the ways in which it bends.

Still, I couldn't deny that the collective power of love surrounding us was a direct factor to Rivs's survival up until this point. It was a phenomenon that defied science and medicine, and even his doctors agreed; in this room, in this sacred space between Rivs's life and what waited around it, something miraculous was occurring.

I began to see a narrowing between what I had learned as a religious child and what I was beginning to find as an adult facing grief once again. Everything I thought I had understood about life, reality, and meaning had dissolved.

In confronting mortality, I realized that I didn't know anything at all. And rather than being unsettled by this undoing, I was freed.

Truth was no longer a choice of divergent paths but rather a kaleidoscope of perspective—an endless variety of patterns depicting the same scene. Everything simply *was*. Despite the polarizing semantics of religion, spirituality, culture, and science, truth was just a twist of the wrist.

Prayer and manifestation, blessings and karma, spirit and energy, god and love, self-betterment and redemption, perfection and acceptance—these terms were synonyms for understanding mortality within the context of eternity. To the ends of the earth and throughout history we'd all been speaking the same language. We were simply using different words.

How liberating it is to be water, fluid and pervious, to flow like love itself—to accept and allow the things we cannot change while moving forward, with love, in the ways we can.

To hear without ears; to speak with closed lips.

* * *

The doctors continued to wake Rivs over the following few weeks, depending on his condition. Sometimes he'd respond by shifting his eyes or lightly squeezing my hand with an index finger, but mostly he'd just lay there.

One afternoon in late August, after Rivs had failed to wake from sedation for seven consecutive days, Dr. Piercecchi stopped me outside the ICU where he was discussing the latest CT scan results with Dr. Briggs. I tried not to notice the way Dr. Briggs was fidgeting nervously with her face shield, or the faint sheen of tears building in Dr. Piercecchi's piercing blue eyes. I had already heard the news: five weeks into treatment, Rivs's scan found only a 50 percent tumor reduction despite three rounds of aggressive chemotherapy. Even worse, Rivs was failing to respond to outside stimuli even though his sedation drips were completely turned off.

"Steph, I'm not sure what condition he'll be in if he wakes up. He's been oxygen deprived for so long now, and we've recently noticed some potential stroke-like episodes." Dr. Piercecchi placed a hand on my shoulder. I could feel the love. "The minutes he spent without oxygen during the ECMO circuit change may have caused severe brain damage. If he makes it through, I want you to be prepared for the possibility that he might not come out of this as the man you once knew."

I nodded. No one was coming out of this unchanged.

Dr. Briggs then turned to me. "The scans show improvement, but not where we were hoping to be this far along in treatment for this particular cancer. Rivs still has a long way to go if we're going to get him off ECMO and start him on the L-asparaginase chemo. We're still walking a tightrope, hoping we can get him well enough to attack the cancer full force. Unfortunately, we're not there yet. Until then, we'll just have to hope his body holds up while we keep cycling him through treatment. I'm sorry I don't have better news."

I nodded again, recognizing the intention behind their words as we stood together in our meeting place between the ICU and the bone marrow transplant unit.

Dr. Piercecchi and Dr. Briggs both wanted him to live as much as I did.

They loved him.

I glanced down at the speckled linoleum floor that separated the ICU and the bone marrow transplant unit. It was a hallway that marked the coming and going of life and death—sick people gurneyed in, dead bodies carted out, bald-headed patients wheeled up and down the floors with someone else's DNA pumping through their rebirthed bodies, each one of them changed by passing through here.

Dr. Briggs leaned against a wall that was decorated with cards for the patients she was trying to save and photographs of the people they once were. And her, the intercessor between sickness and health, life and death.

I looked around. I could finally see it.

This hallway feels so different from when I first arrived—back when I was a visitor in the space between living and dying. But I live here now. Here in the now where these two doors are less like a gulf and more like a bridge. The vastness between them is far less lonely than I once believed.

This hallway, with its knowing floors and walls of eternal memorandum—the one I walk in fear and anger and sorrow and gratitude and love—is no longer a cruel and lonely separation.

It is a path.

A torii.

A river flowing from mundane to sacred, sacred to mundane and back, over and over again.

Nothing is ever lost in these halls, no matter how they are left.

There is so much awareness in the interim, so much held in between. In this staccatoed knowing that echoes infinitely, life and death are not worlds apart. They are a chorus with no beginning and no end, each of them bending inward like time, undeniably and inextricably linked.

I can finally hear it. In the melody of eternity, life and death are simply fermatas to an infinite refrain.

Though silent in the pause, there is no void between them—just a prolonging of awareness.

As Dr. Briggs spoke of sickness and health, I realized that duality was simply a finite definition for all the grayness my human mind could not yet understand.

Where once everything felt linear, now it was all round. Everything had been taught to me in black and white, but the world was really just gray, gray, gray, gray. Even Rivs's treatment was an example of this wholeness, a practical case being made before my eyes: everything in existence needed a contradictory appendage to move forward. Life and death, overmedication and undertreatment, too much oxygen and not enough, consciousness and rest—no thing was complete without an opposing auxiliary. Not even life itself. Perhaps meaning wasn't found on either side of these poles, but in the spaces between them.

Pain and joy, beauty and terror, then and now: these experiences were not oppositional but complementary, necessary in the grand unsnarling of existence. And if these experiences were indeed complementary, then it was plausible that all emotions could be felt simultaneously.

I wondered whether this was the true significance in attributing the divine power of suffering to Jesus—a paradigmatic lesson teaching that both divinity and humanness are found in feeling everything all at once. In this very human ability, despite our limited view of the world that would separate us from god, despite teachings that would remove us from our propensity to experience the wholeness of each moment, each one of us is inherently divine.

In our ability to suffer and experience joy in the same breath—in our potential to exist infinitely in each moment, to straddle life and death and accept it all as one cyclical round, gray and weightless, heavy and beautiful—we are both god and human.

Through death, life was revealing to me that god was not found in black and white but in the beauty and terror of gray. Better was not adherence to rules but the ability to meet myself with love. Perfect was not the absence of sin but the acceptance of my brokenness, to love it all—light and dark and all the spaces between them.

That afternoon, I thanked Dr. Piercecchi for his constant commitment to keeping Rivs alive. I expressed gratitude to Dr. Briggs for trusting Rivs enough to know she could put him through hell for the chance that he might come out to see the light one day.

He was running the canyon at night but he was no longer afraid of the dark. Maybe he never had been. Maybe he'd always seen right through it—and maybe I'd always been right there beside him, lighting the way with my love.

Nothing had changed. I could just see it differently now.

I said goodbye to Dr. Briggs and Dr. Piercecchi, leaving the hospital with a burning memory, something that had been kindling in my soul all my life, or maybe longer. A lesson I had been taught over and over again but was only now beginning to remember. A simple truth that had been whispered many times but I was only now hearing: *God is love and love is gray.*

In transcending the confines of polarity, I was beginning to understand the fullness of human existence, which in its truest sense, is love.

Love is uniquely happening always, right now. It is perhaps the only experience that can exist without contradiction, without an opposing force.

Other than light, love was the only element I could think of that evaded relativity—consistent regardless of intention, stable despite what came towards it, unchanged through turbulence. Though the circumstance surrounding love might change or eventually fade, the notion persisted, if only as a memory. Something we'd always known to be true.

Maybe this was life in essence, time in its shrouded malleability. All of life was a microcosmic round as the universe begged me to listen to its only message, *none of it matters but love*. How you learn this, be it through religion, science, psychedelics, meditation, physical exertion, service, or pain, is secondary to arriving here, at the point.

And that point—the meaning, the purpose, the reason, all of it? It was love. Pure and unrequited. The only thing that existed on both sides of the pendulum and the only thing found in the awareness between them.

Pain was my conduit to love. It felt like an acute lesson now as I navigated Rivs's illness, but in looking back I'd see that this truth had been unwinding over the years, looping on repeat, playing quietly in the background of my life until I was ready to hear it.

Did this attribute inherent meaning to my suffering or some noble reason for tragedy? No. Even as the course of Rivs's treatment played out with seeming serendipity, I still did not believe that everything happened for a reason. That sort of projection felt dangerous, the inclination to assign moral significance to suffering. What then, of the countless people around the globe enduring far worse tragedies than this? What of entire nations raised in generational starvation, oppression, and war? What of a parent grieving a child? Even in agony I saw my pain as microscopic in comparison. Though I understood the relativity of suffering, I knew I was in no position to assign meaning to anyone else's.

Sometimes, pain is entirely tragic.

But in softness I found my strength. In my brokenness I found a voice. In pain I found love. In darkness I saw flashes of blinding light. In the wake of my father's death, I learned incredible empathy—for my mother, for my daughters, for the world, for myself. And in that grief I learned that all of it—the good, the bad, the anger, the joy—all of it is incomplete without its opposite.

Everything, except love.

As far as I could tell, love was the only singular human emotion. The only thing that could uniquely exist everywhere and in isolation all at once. Without beginning, without end, without the necessity for preface or polarity.

The only thing in this world that is truly pure and purely true.

And in that singularity, I found god.

Which is to say, I found myself.

AND WHILE YOU SLEEP I AWAKE

August 22, 2020

They say you are finally dying. The doctors tell me they can feel it and maybe I can, too. When I left your bedside last night I didn't sense you close to me like I normally do. For the first time in all of this, you were far away.

Unreachable.

I guess even in the medical world there is gray; a sense of the unempirical, the intangible—a place no one can define but some can feel. I know this because I felt it, too. Even before Dr. Pierecchi called to give me the evening update, I knew.

You are no longer here.

For the first time in six weeks, you are nowhere. I can't find you. Once again I'm searching like a child waking from a dream, looking for something that was just right here.

Weren't you just right here?

Interesting, isn't it, how the body remains but we can still sense the departure.

There must be something to that. Strange that after all these years it's death that has shown me the miracle of life. Yes, I said miracle. I know, Rivs. I know . . . There's just no other word for it, is there? The fullness of life supersedes biological existence. Being alive is a marriage of spirit and science. It's truly a miracle. I know you see it now, too.

Today when I left you, your mouth was twisted open like you'd said everything you'd needed to say in this life. Your eyes were rolled back in your head like you had seen enough of this world. I've seen that face before. But that wasn't even why I knew you were gone.

I knew because when I leaned my forehead against yours, gently, so as not to move you, I couldn't hear you at all. Maybe discernment is a miracle, too. Not the kind we pray for, but a miracle, still. I'm starting to see them everywhere, you know.

Yesterday they turned off all of your sedation again and you spent the whole day still, still, still, both in this world and the space in between. I listened for you but you were nowhere to be found.

It was a sight and a sound all too familiar to me and you *know* this, Rivs. You know this.

How could you do that to me? How could you die like that? How could you die like *this*, exactly this?

I know you fought hard for me and the girls, but I still want to yell "FUCK YOU" into your pale and withered face.

And maybe while I'm at it, I'll yell that at my dad, too, because at least now I know he can hear me.

Fuck you, both of you, for leaving me.

Is that strange?

Did you know you'd leave me behind? Did you know you can mourn two people in one body? When I used to tell you stories about navigating the world fatherless, did you know you'd one day do the same to your own daughters?

Did you?

It's seven thirty on a Thursday morning and I'm driving to you, like I've done every day for the past forty-seven days. I haven't missed a single morning with you. Do you see, now, how much I love you? Can you finally feel all the love we couldn't see with open eyes?

Dr. Piercecchi called last night to tell me he doesn't think you'll make it much longer, that you've taken a turn for the worst even after how far you've come. This latest round of chemo is scouring your body from the inside out. Everything about you is slowing down now, after weeks of hanging on.

"Sometimes people just get tired of fighting. Even Rivs," he said with more affection than I'd ever imagined a doctor to have. When the hospice nurse told me to let my dad go all those years ago it felt a little less sincere. Or maybe that's just how I remembered it.

Can you see how much people love you, Rivs?

Anyway, the will to leave inevitably escapes us, the body gives in, and no amount of love can save it. I know this all too well.

Love is an anchor but sometimes not enough to tether us to this world.

You've been in the hospital for almost two months now and it's the first time I've believed them when they've said that it's time to say goodbye, that it's time to prepare the girls to come in and see you, if that's something we choose for them. *We.* As if there's any joint decision-making anymore. They're asking me to tell your family—maybe your dad can fly in before you take your last breath?

Even though you might not know it, you've endured two rounds of chemotherapy since we last spoke face to face. Wait—did you even know that you have cancer? Well, plot twist, babe. You're dying of mother-fucking lung cancer. Yeah, I know. The irony. It's almost funny, isn't it?

Yeah, almost.

The day is just beginning for me. What does time feel like where you are? Iris and Harper just logged on to their online classes and Poppy is wearing a little green apron, helping the grandmas make pancakes. My mum has been cooking the girls hot breakfast every single morning, letting them top off on whipped cream and shake their own sprinkles on perfectly round pancakes. Not too many, but still. Every morning, babe. How am I going to break that habit when life gets back to normal?

Normal. Ha!

Last night I asked Dr. Piercecchi how much time you had left—whether it would be hours or days. He said days, maybe a few, so I'm coming in, one last time, before I let the girls see you. He says you're tired. So tired. Maybe I need to see for myself before I decide to relive the experience of seeing a dead father from a mother's perspective before allowing our children to see their own.

Do you want to know something funny, Rivs? Other than knowing that our girls will grow up without a dad, the saddest part of this whole fucking tragedy is the fact that I won't be able to talk to you about it later, that I won't be able to laugh about your nurses' idiosyncrasies or tease you for your stubbornness after the girls go to bed.

Will you ever know how strong I was? Do you remember how hard I fought to get you to the hospital that night? Did you know that I didn't even panic, that I just fucking did it?

Do you know that in your impending death I found my own strength? What are the fucking chances?

Is it romantic or pathetic that I still need your validation? Even after discovering all the power inside me, I'm still so desperate for your love.

Why didn't you go to the hospital earlier, Rivs?

Why?

Why didn't I insist?

I'm stepping out of the elevator now. I just waved to Fringa—she's making her way down the hall towards the ICU, her yellow mop bucket trailing behind her. I hope she has someone at home who loves her.

What is it about love, anyways?

Here I am now, waving my hand through the narrow window that looks into the ICU from the BMT hallway. I have a smile on my face. It's contrived but sincere, somehow. I'm hoping that someone at the nurses' station will see me and let me in so I don't have to get a key from reception.

I'm walking towards your room now. I see the back of your head peeking up from behind your bed. I always see the top of your bald head first, through the windows of your swinging doors, the ones that have signs taped all over them, like "Chemotherapy Precaution," "ECMO," and "Do Not Move Patient."

I'm walking in and I can see that your body isn't jerking for breath like it normally is, which is good because it means you're not struggling for air, but it also means that the ventilator is breathing for you. How does that saying go—we're living until we stop moving? Something like that.

Anyways, I'm beside you now. I'm looking down at you. Your teeth are so perfect and white. It was one of the first things I noticed about you in Anthropology class. Did I ever tell you that?

Have you had enough, Rivs?

Are you really done?

If you are, I understand. I do. And I'm not actually mad at you. I don't really want to scream "fuck you" in your face. My dad's face, either. In fact, now that I'm staring at you, it's the last thing I'd ever want to do.

I'm just so sad, Rivs. I'm so sad. Isn't it strange that sadness often comes as rage when it's rooted in love? Isn't it true that we can hold all of those things at once?

Do me a favor—remind me of that down the road, when our girls are teenagers. Will you come to me in the space in between, somehow, and remind me of that? I promise I'll be listening for you. Remind me that despite it all I turned out okay? Oh, babe, my poor mum. I was such a mess for her. Such a fucking mess, and she just loved me through it. She let me move freely in my anger. Remind me of that, too.

I'm sitting next to you now. You look so far away—tired but still so beautiful. You're the love of my life, Rivs. I hope you know that. I'm sorry I didn't show you that enough when you were alive. I'm sorry life always seemed so hard for you. You weren't really meant for this world, were you? I can see that now. You've always been a spirit in the space in between.

I'm sorry you had to fight so hard to live this long, and I don't mean just since being sick. I'm sorry I put you through all of this. I just couldn't imagine a life without you in it.

I'm laying my hands on your bare chest now, right above the plastic tube that sticks out from between your ribs. I don't really know why but I'm doing it. I'm closing my eyes and bowing my head towards you, and I can see myself now—a fourteen-year-old grieving her dying father. It is a pain low and growling and desperate. And now it's Harper I see. Can you believe she's about to turn eleven? Fuck, babe, she's so lost and afraid without you.

And I'm beginning to feel something now. It's not you, but it's something. Or is it someone?

I'm recalling a memory of truth, a concept I've always known. It's there on the periphery but coming into focus, slowly. Something or someone is giving me this knowing, silent and resounding.

Here it is:

I cannot say goodbye to you. Not right now. Not like this.

I need to keep you here.

For Harper.

For me at fourteen.

I hear it. I feel it. I know it.

I'm clawing to you, now. I'm taking off my flip-flops and planting my bare feet on the ground. I'm not sure why or how but I'm making my way to you. Do you see me? Can you hear me? You're so far away. This place is an echoing chamber of everything all at once and I don't know where you are. For the first time, I can't find you.

Stay here, Rivs. *Stay*. There's nowhere better.

My hands are stretched flat across your chest now. My palms are wide but I'm clawing. I'm clawing, babe. I'm tearing through the cosmos.

Who knew you could travel so far while sitting still? Who knew you could hurt in places outside your body?

And oh—here she is. I'm staring death in the face. I feel her hot breath down my neck. *I know you well.* I'm lifting my right arm to the square. I'm using my voice. *Do you hear me?* I'm roaring:

"NO. You can't have him this time."

But the words that come out are this:

Iris, Poppy, Harper. Iris, Poppy, Harper. Iris, Poppy, Harper.

Can you feel it, Rivs? Find your way back to us.

Remember.

There is a beacon flashing in the ether. It is love.

Love is the light.

I know everything is round and warm where you are, in the place above time and space, but you need to remember that we're here all around it, waiting for you.

Remember.

Draw the pieces in and come back to us. The roundness will be waiting but right now you need to be here, where time moves forward, where little girls grow up and grieve.

We're all standing here, waiting.

Iris, Poppy, Harper. Iris, Poppy, Harper. Iris, Poppy, Harper.

Do you remember when we first met—how I had to ask you to kiss me? You were so shy, babe. So shy. Do you remember how we used to let Harper sleep in a hammock outside our little house in Costa Rica? How we eventually moved the couch onto the front porch so we could take turns pushing her because she wouldn't sleep in that crib you built from the mango tree in our yard? Do you remember when you cut Iris's bangs so short we weren't sure if she looked more like Harper Lee or a barista from Portland, or when Poppy used to rescue the feeder mice from Harper's pet snake, and she'd crawl around the house, clutching them to death in her tiny palm?

Remember, babe. I know you're everywhere right now but try. Try to be here. Memory is a language, too. It moors us. Try to remember.

Iris, Poppy, Harper. Iris, Poppy, Harper.

What is it about love, anyways?

Iris, Poppy, Harper. Iris, Poppy, Harper.

We were always searching for meaning in hidden places, but it really is so simple, isn't it?

Iris, Poppy, Harper. Iris, Poppy, Harper.

I can hear you now, so faint I can barely feel it but you're calling me to you.

No, Rivs, I can't go where you are. The roundness doesn't allow linear beings like me.

You want to take me somewhere? Well, maybe just for a moment. A moment or forever, or both.

We're in Hawaii now. It's late at night and you're asking me to dance in front of your house, the one you lived in when we first met. We were just kids back then, weren't we? Two barefoot kids and the grass is soft and wet. It's squishing between my toes so I put them up on yours, and now we're moving together. Two people, one body. It's always felt like that to me. Is that so bad? Does that make me less of a woman, to want to be so deeply at one with a man? I'm beginning to believe that the right kind of love gives us power, not the other way around. We shouldn't have to choose between the two.

The stars are so clear tonight. So clear you can almost see it, can't you? The everythingness of it all.

We're really here, aren't we? In Hawaii? This isn't a dream—it's a memory of something happening right now, and something that's happened a million times before. I can feel it. We're really here, together. Maybe this is what soulmate means—a memory of love that plays on repeat throughout eternity with no beginning, no end. And if you look hard enough, you can always find it.

You're pulling me in close and I'm resting my head on your chest. There's no music but we're dancing, slowly. You're singing me a Mason Jennings song, softly, your lips pressed against my forehead.

If you need a reason as to why you're here, you don't need to look farther than me.

Our wedding song. I always loved hearing you sing it. I wish you sang more often.

I nestle my head harder into your chest. It's strong and unbridled. No tubes, no lines, no machines. Just you. I want to remember you this way.

I want to remember how you once loved life so fully. How you once loved me so fully. How you once loved yourself.

And just as abruptly as you found me, you have to leave.

Thank you for dancing with me, you say.

I'll be back tomorrow, I reply. *Please don't forget that everything you ever need is right here. I love you, now, in this moment, which is also forever. And you always come back. Remember?*

I'll try, you say. And then you're gone.

I'm opening my eyes now and it feels like I'm waking up from the deepest sleep. What time is it? I've been with you for four hours but we lived lifetimes together, didn't we?

I'm driving home now. I feel sick, like I pulled something out of you. I pulled it out of your body and it went through me, up through my palms and out through my bare feet into the ground. I've offered you the resounding truth I had to learn through your deaths.

Everything you need is right here. Everything I need is right here.

I park the car to vomit but after a few breaths I find I'm able to hold it until I get back home.

I stumble through the front door and find my way to Harper's bedroom, where she is fast asleep. I crawl in next to her, wrap my arms around her growing body and put my lips to her forehead. She's getting so big, Rivs. Time doesn't pause here.

Tomorrow when I walk into your room you will greet me with a tired smile. Your nurses will bring all the doctors in to see it. The world will blur around us but your eyes will be locked on mine, knowing.

You remembered.

You are awake.

* * *

Hi, Dad. I'm sorry I didn't hear you before. I can hear you now, in the spaces between, in that very real place I've come to know so well.

It was you all along, wasn't it?

You were always just right here.

I see the miracle now.

Marc, Solomon, Bishop Huang, Craig, Fringa, Dr. Piercecchi, the voice—weren't they all you?

Weren't they all me?

Aren't we all, in our purest forms, love?

I remember now.

We were always everything, all at once.

I remember.

I am awake.

THE ECMO DIARIES

Writing has always been my means of understanding the world. When Rivs was sedated and put on a ventilator on July 16, 2020, I started recording my thoughts and feelings to cope with the tragedy before me. I began posting my reflections on Instagram as a way of updating the thousands of people who had stepped forward to help our family throughout the course of his illness. In response to my writing, I was met with more love and support than I could have ever imagined.

In many ways, I was saved by the online community that rallied around me during the darkest time of my life.

These are my thoughts, in chronological order.

||||||||||||||||||||||||||

JULY 16, 2020

"The wound is where the light comes in."

—Rumi

A voice in my ear, real and true as I tossed and turned in my bed last night: *This is not how he dies.* My mind goes to dark places when it comes to sickness. When I was six, my three-year-old brother was diagnosed with leukemia. When I was thirteen, my dad was diagnosed with adenocarcinoma (lung cancer) and died a year later. A few years after that, my older brother was diagnosed with testicular cancer. And now, with

Rivs in the ICU with a yet-unknown lung disease, my mind can't help but careen into places it shouldn't go. If grief was a leaky roof, I'd say I've had my tin filled, haunted for years by the ting-ting-ting of water filling a pail. But life doesn't work in weight and measure—there is no cap on pain. The bucket just gets bigger. Sometimes there is more grief than we feel we can handle—it overflows whatever pail we've used to catch the leak. It seeps out of us, onto the floors, up the walls, out the windows. For a little while, we drown. It's dark.

And then, the light shines through—weak at first, like the subtle smell of spring you can taste before you can see. You reach your hand up to see if it's real. Light glows through your fingers. There it is, out of the abyss, gleaning in on the horizon: hope, healing, a way forward.

Rivs is strong. He is a fighter. He is the love of our lives. He will help me see the light shining in.

‖‖‖‖‖‖‖‖‖‖‖‖‖‖‖‖‖‖‖

JULY 30, 2020

I open my computer to write and there you are, haunting this blank screen. The cursor pulses. It taunts me. What is there to write about other than you? What will there ever be? The hyperbolic pause that blinks as I wait. An exaggerated breath that I understand in all its cruel irony.

The pendulum swings and the fear of your absence consumes me. Hope and defeat. Here and there. Now and later. Will we grow old together? Will you see the trees you planted in April sprout their leaves next spring? Will we see the redwoods like we said we would?

If tragedy is a well then uncertainty is a bucket at the end of a tattered rope. The comfort of the well lies in knowing your fate. In the bucket you can reach out, hang on to tenacious strings that speak of maybe, that tell of faith and miracles. But hope hurts and faith is vulnerable, leaving you in the tidal chance of making it out.

An inexorable uncertainty. An unending maybe. It clots and claws.

It is tepid down here, in the maybe. I reach for the rope but it burns my hand as I lose my grip. It's easier to float in the dark well of finality. To root out the hope that burrows.

"Ignore the bucket. Ignore the rope. There is no way out. You've done this before and it didn't end well."

So is this it—the apex of the maelstrom? You thought you'd reached it in your teens. You thought that was the depth of it. You thought you'd reached the pinnacle of despair.

"Oh, girl," he whispers. "The darkness is so much wider."

And who are you, anyways? Who is it that haunts me now— father or lover, demon or deity? The lines have been blurred my whole life. Blessings and trials. Lessons and burdens. Promises of eternity that end in early departure. You left when I was young. Will you leave me again? Impermanence becomes permanent.

The bucket, the rope. The water, the well. The pendulum swings.

||||||||||||||||||||||||||

AUGUST 3, 2020

Rivs woke up for a bit today. It was the first time in two weeks that I knew he could hear me—really hear me. It was beautiful and it was tragic. Nothing can prepare you for it, the murky eyes, the sunken cheeks, the recognition, the desperation, the heartache, the beauty. "You're in the hospital. You can't talk, yet. But you will. You will. Just relax. I'm here. I love you." So many words unspoken. So many questions left unanswered. A palm in hand, another stroking his head. There you were, and here you are. You're doing it. For now, that's all.

There is life and there is death, but there is so much in between. So much hanging on the precipice when you're unsure which is closer.

But I believe that Rivs is closer to life. I saw it in his eyes as they searched for me, in his lips that moved and tried to make meaning, in the tear that rolled down his cheek when I told him Iris was about to lose her second tooth.

"If this was anyone else on earth, they would not be here now. But here we are, improving every day with a long-term plan. He is truly incredible. What a remarkable feat." That is what the oncologist told me today.

Small deposits. Tiny miracles unfolding before my eyes— miracles I had written off decades ago.

Life is fragile. The skull grins in. The pendulum swings. Life and death. And so much in between.

ıılıllılllılllılllllllllll

AUGUST 7, 2020

He keeps fighting. He's in it now—the storm before the relative calm. They told us he would get worse before he gets better, and here we are. I sit beside him and watch his chest heave. I see him struggle to get oxygen, even with all of the life-saving devices coming and going from his beautiful body. He is fighting. It is palpable. I wish I could do more. It's a special kind of hell, I think. This helplessness. And then his doctor says, as if reading my mind, "You know, you're as important in this puzzle as we are, if not more." I squeeze Rivs's hand a little tighter.

He was tired yesterday. I went home and recorded the girls' voices living life as normal, whatever that means anymore. I brought those sounds to him today as he slept. I hope it helps. And as they played, our wedding song, by Mason Jennings, came to mind.

"If you need a reason as to why you're here, you don't need to look farther than me."

Keep doing it, Rivs.

||||||||||||||||||||||||

AUGUST 8, 2020

How do you put it into words? The pain. The pain. It is so deep. It's so tragic, and still, so beautiful. He looks at me and smiles. From the hollows of pain he emerges with light. If only for a moment, he shines. The painful paradox of life that now rages day and night. Day and night.

We can't recognize joy without pain.

"At least it's not a child," I tell myself. Consolation for a desperate soul. It comforts. It could be worse.

In the eye of the storm and I already know at least one good thing will come from this devastation, either way it leads: I will learn a greater empathy.

Life is good until it isn't, and it is in these moments we learn how to love. From the depths of sorrow sprouts a beautiful truth: we are not alone in pain. We are a network—roots connected in sadness and growing out of darkness towards the light.

||||||||||||||||||||||||

AUGUST 13, 2020

Life is fragile but people are resilient. And still, the machines beep, the alarms sound, the blood drips in even while it gets drawn out over, and over, and over again. I sit here and watch it flow through tubes—out from his body and into a tiny, miraculous machine that pulls out carbon dioxide and infuses oxygen as his lungs fail. There is an acute awareness here. A heavy reckoning of humility—it is two machines, a team of brilliant doctors, and a slew of medicine keeping him alive. This is vulnerability. This is reverent devotion to science, to medicine, to technology, to great minds. A bowing to faith in things I do not understand. Maybe this is where I reconcile with the divine. Spirit, magic, energy, medicine.

Last night, while putting a third cannula in through Rivs's femoral vein to increase ECMO blood flow, a large air bubble was sucked into the system and stopped the circuit. For a few minutes, Rivs was left without this life support. The medical team reacted quickly, and here he is today. Alive, fighting, and raging on.

Here is the divine.

Now I sit next to him as his heart beats, his lungs inflate, his eyes flutter open now and then, and I think, over and over: life is fragile but people are resilient. Pain is deep but love endures. Hope hurts but miracles happen. The pendulum, the paradox. The duality of existence that makes life so tragic and still, so beautiful.

⸻⸻⸻

AUGUST 16, 2022

"Poppy, Iris, Harper. Poppy, Iris, Harper."

I whisper their names into your ear like a prayer. Or is it a battle cry?

I wonder whether it's softness or adamance that keeps the spirit going. I do not know, so I reach for both. I draw them in like coming up for air.

I remember a conversation we had about these things, maybe a week before you got sick. Softness and strength. I sit next to you today and think "this is you, right now, resting gently with the strength of a warrior." Even as you sleep, you teach me.

Here is strength in all its softness. Softness in all its strength. And it is powerful.

The way you were meant to be.

And as you lie, I whisper their names, softly. There is a desperation in there—one that comes from a lifetime of knowing that time does not heal all wounds.

The chest heaves, the machines beep, the medicine drips in. I nestle my hand under yours. I feel the warmth that I've come to appreciate as a miracle. I cry when I need to, laugh with your nurses if I feel like it.

I do not know if this is strength, but it's all I have.

I think you feel the same.

⁣⁣⁣⁣⁣⁣⁣⁣⁣⁣⁣⁣⁣⁣⁣⁣⁣⁣⁣⁣⁣

AUGUST 18, 2020

Last night I had a dream that you were sinking in quicksand. I reached in with both my hands to pull you out but still you slipped under. I awoke before knowing if you made it, if my strength was enough to rescue you.

That's how life is right now. Unknowing, uncertainty. Slipping, grasping, sinking. Moments of unbridled hope mixed with utter despair. More pendulum, more paradox.

Some days it feels like floating and others it feels like drowning. I swear the hyperbole alone will kill me.

Some days you're scared. I can see it in your eyes and it haunts me. You're asking me to save you but I don't know how. You're sinking and there's no way to pull you out. I grasp for something to tether me, to give me leverage. "Is there more medicine you can give him?" I ask. I try to subdue the desperation in my voice. I want to be strong for you but I feel so weak, like I might be sinking too. Sometimes I rub your head or sing a song we both know but I still can't drag you out. I'm trying but I just can't.

Some days I send you messages—memes I think you'll laugh

at, quotes that might inspire you, photos that will make you smile. Last night I sent a message that broke my heart.

"I miss you babe."

Because I do. I just do, Rivs. For all the ups and downs, all the somedays in between, amidst hope and despair, for all the paradox and poetry and punctuation that studs my thoughts with feigned eloquence to mar the devastation—the only constant is this simple message, whether you're sinking or rising, whether I'm floating or drowning. Wherever we are on this pendulum swing, I miss you. Every day. I miss you.

‖‖‖‖‖‖‖‖‖‖‖‖‖‖‖‖‖‖

AUGUST 21, 2020

Where have you been? Where did you go while you were asleep? I'd like to imagine you were bending time and space, falling back onto the sands of Puerto Rico while Poppy and Harper jumped from the dock, Iris nuzzled into your chest. Or maybe you've been dancing with me under a night sky, singing softly in my ear. Time seems less cruel when I think of you this way.

But where are you now, as you wake up? Neither here nor there, it seems. You are liminal. Fumes from an exhaust pipe dissipating into thin air. Tangible and then unseen. Nothing can prepare you for it. I say it again and again, in writing and then out loud. "Nothing can prepare you for this."

Eyes searching, chest heaving, mouth bleeding, that swing between calm and panic. Calm and panic.

They tell me you might not be in there anymore. For over a month you've been lying in a bed, filled with narcotics and robbed of oxygen. Time is a cruel captor when it does not bend.

But I see. There is so much life left in you. It seeps through your pores even as you sleep. I see it in the way your eyebrows raise when I say your name—the way your eyes search for my voice, only mine. I see the way your mouth widens into an open-mouthed smile when you hear me play Iris's sweet voice. "I love you, Dad."

I see you.

You may be neither here nor there, but then again, you've always been that way. Straddling that fine line between joy and pain, life and death. On the brink, always. You know this world of in-between. At times it has been your home. Just please come back to ours.

IIIIIIIIIIIIIIIIIIIIIIIIIII

AUGUST 24, 2020

Here you are. I felt it before I saw it. Sometimes, or maybe often, the spirit speaks louder than words. So much can be said with a heart opened by the humility of pain.

"I'm still here."

I saw you before you even opened your eyes. I heard you before you opened your lips. I am learning through experience the things I've read in books—there is more power in the spaces in between. There is more said in the inhale if we listen to the calm, the interlude between acts. That quiet pause of reflection where we take it all in and prepare for the script to play out.

Eyes closed, head bowed, hands feeling before seeing.

"I'm still here" and "Did you ever doubt me?"

This is faith. This, right here, is hope. Not a cloud in the sky, not an everlasting kingdom, not X-rays or numbers on a screen. It's a power, a knowing that transcends consciousness, that supersedes science and rationale. It speaks in the staccatos of awareness, the space in which we are most present.

Love. All love.

Here you are, tethered by it, rooted to this world by love amidst the chaos. Not trapped but grounded by the spaces between.

I hear you.

||||||||||||||||||||||||||

AUGUST 28, 2020

Eyes. Those eyes. A recurring villain in my life. They tell of distance, of runaway trains, of spaces too far between.

They speak volumes in their vacancy. I've seen those eyes before. Time has made a master out of me.

My dad had those same eyes when he was sick—the ones that look through you, past you, into the distance with the faintest hint of nostalgia.

"Hello, old friend. Don't I know you from somewhere?"

So this is where I feel you more than I see you. This is the space in between that we now share. We live here, for now.

And here is where I push past the cynicism of tragedy, the one I lived two decades ago. Here is where I am grateful to have seen those eyes before because I know life lives beyond them, behind them, between them. Even after them.

Can you be grateful for tragedy? I think so. Here I am, holding your hand and finding comfort in those eyes. The ones I've seen before. The ones that greeted me as a dinner guest when I was his fucking daughter. The ones that saw past me a little too long.

But you're still here, Rivs. Your story is not my father's. Your story doesn't end the same way.

And though you come and go, I stay. I take the train to wherever you're going, knowing you will come back.

A distant gaze, and then you make a joke. A glassy stare, and then a smile.

Here you are again. Thank you for coming back to me.

||||||||||||||||||||||||

SEPTEMBER 6, 2020

It takes work to stay alive—to build a life and keep it, too. I spend most of my days sitting beside a man whose life relies on two machines, hourly blood tests, and medically calculated titrations.

Blood pressure, tidal volumes, pH balance, platelets, hemoglobin, respiratory rates, cardiac output, carbon dioxide sweep, ATP, magnesium, calcium, phosphorus.

The words we never have to think about when things are going well are the things that keep us alive.

It is a truly sobering experience to watch the pageantry behind keeping a body in this world. To watch the brilliance, love, care, and meticulous attention to detail it takes to play god.

It makes me realize just how much I take for granted. It makes me appreciate what it means to live. To breathe. To sit upright and eat a meal. To thoughtlessly allow my body to self-regulate, to exchange life-sustaining gases, to pump blood at the right rate.

And this is just the baseline mechanics of staying alive. It doesn't even touch on what it means to live: to love, to hurt and feel and scream and laugh and cry. To look someone in the eye and see them. *Truly* see them. To be conscious and aware. To know where you are and why. To open a hand and close it. To wiggle your toes on demand.

I've never liked the word "miraculous." It's a term I abandoned years ago, when I was being stoked by the flames of anger.

I've never been one to cling to the notion of eternity in order to assuage my fear of death. I am still unclear on where I stand on the bridge between this world and the next, if there is one at all.

But here I am today, saying: What a miracle it is to be alive. Here. Now.

How incredible it is that we *live*.

There must be something divine in it. There has to be

something that supersedes our understanding of biological existence. Somewhere in the cosmos there was a marriage of spirit and science.

And it was rare. And it was beautiful.

It was a miracle.

||||||||||||||||||||||||

SEPTEMBER 9, 2020

Who are you now, Rivs? In what ways will you be different after this? In the midst of uncertainty comes at least one absolute: there is no way we come out of this unchanged.

Tragedy shapes us for better or worse. It molds us like clay. We are spun in the depths of despair and then forged in the kiln of awareness.

That is where we were, dizzied and confused. We were malleable and didn't even know it. We didn't understand how far we could bend without breaking until we were thrown.

And here we are now, either burning with anger or setting with new resolve. It is up to us to decide whether we grow or decay. It is our choice to crumble or be made stronger by the hands of circumstance.

Exactly a year ago today, you and I were on a plane to Japan, leafing through a Japanese guidebook. Of all the beautiful artistry, philosophical mantras, and breathtaking scenery, one idea that resonated most with you was the concept of kintsukuroi: the art of repairing pottery with gold or silver lacquer and understanding that the piece is more beautiful after having been broken.

I look at you, Rivs. I see the road ahead. It is one filled with frustration, sickness, and pain. At times it seems an implacable cycle of defeat. It is a broken road. But it is also a furnace of reinvention, if we allow it. There is a space between fire and glaze where we decide how to set.

I can't say who I'll be after this. There are days I float in sadness, listless in that sinking calm. Other days I reach for anger's hand, fueled by her flame when the pain is too deep to navigate alone. Gratitude and bitterness pull at me. "I see you both," I say. "You each have a place."

I don't know where our cracks are, or how deep they will be.

All I know is that in those fissures is a choice: dwell in the sadness that caused them, or be fortified by the love that will make us whole again.

||||||||||||||||||||||||||

SEPTEMBER 12, 2020

"This is wild."

One of Rivs's most audible statements since being able to speak.

I have moments of clarity—when the image of who you are versus who you were converges into a strange current of the present. It is trickling at first—a thought will catch me, usually instigated by a photo. The curve of your bicep, the strength in your smile, the resolve in your eyes the way they used to be.

And then, a cascading force of reckoning with the now.

You are sick. So sick.

Last night I saw a photo of you bearded, strong, and resilient. It brought me to my knees but only because I allowed it. I've learned to keep at bay the intersection of truths—the then and now. It is only in these stark contrasts that I recognize the tragedy before us—in the presence of expectation.

Your body is frail. Your eyes are wide and searching. Your awareness comes and goes.

How can a mountain become a valley? How does a river become a stream?

It is hard to see you dependent. The greatest tragedy is witnessing the vacancy in your eyes.

So I dam the thoughts. I divert the flood to save myself. All there is is now. All you've ever been is right in front of me.

But last night, while I allowed myself to be swept away in the rapids, there it was. Something *real*.

Rivs, you are the confluence. You are the meeting of then and now. Here, as you wake up to this new you. Not less but more. Stronger for having both past and present flowing through you. Into you. Between you.

Who you were and who you are may seem divergent. The delta of tragedy split you in two, and right now it might seem like you've been weakened by it.

And yet, here you are. Different, yes, but still a river carving your way through basalt. And at the end is a powerful convergence flowing relentlessly forward towards what is to come. No matter what, nothing can stop it.

We might try to diffuse the grief on a floodplain. It seems more tolerable than the quagmire of sorrow. But I saw it last night. I will try to see it every day.

Your body is weak and your eyes might be searching, but you are even stronger here, as the confluence of then and now.

You are a torrent of reckoning. A relentless groundbreaking current.

And you're right: it is wild.

||||||||||||||||||||||||

SEPTEMBER 19, 2020

He is going to live.

It is a bold statement—one that feels like stepping on thin ice, delicate and tentative. It is safer to stay on the banks of realism, harbored by the surety of past experience. I want to cling on for fear it won't be true, from the knowledge that believing can be a frigid plunge.

But something coaxes me towards you.

A lighthouse on the horizon.

I see you now, gleaming in hallowed ombrés. Distant and obscured by fog, but there you are.

Across the frozen water you call to me.

"It's safe to walk," you say. "She is strong enough to hold your weight."

You've always been there, haven't you? Shining through the thick of it though I was moored by anger and fear.

If only I had strained my eyes to see.

And she has always been strong enough to hold my weight, hasn't she? She never broke at all.

If only I had realized it was *me* who cracked.

So I walk towards you now, sure footed with eyes on the horizon.

Because she can hold the weight of it.

Hope.

And you call to us, day and night.

Light.

He is going to live.

||||||||||||||||||||||||||

SEPTEMBER 23, 2020

Seventy days.

They blur together in a fog. Or do they shatter like glass? I can't tell whether the last two months have been melting together or cracking apart.

Is this fissure or fusion?

The days are divided into good or bad. At the end of each day I gather up our experiences and try to put them in little boxes. Binary is easier to process. The gray that I've so passionately advocated for isn't found here.

You still come and go. It is good or it is bad. On the days you can breathe, your mind is away, floating in the space between that both holds and haunts us. On the days you are alert, you struggle with oxygen. You say you feel like you're drowning.

I feel ungrateful for complaining when the trajectory has been upward, and still, these days are hard. The bad ones—when you don't see me. When your eyes look past me, or beg me to take you with me when I leave.

Seventy days of good and bad, worse and better. Seventy days I've tried to categorize my feelings when they're everything, all at once.

The water, the well, the bucket, the rope, the fog, the ice, the river, the rage, the banks, the lighthouse, the broken glass, the confluence.

It seems we are both fighting an ineffable battle between the world outside us and the world within—one we can't quite describe. We try to grasp the pendulum somewhere in the middle, try to weigh it down at some semblance of six o'clock, but it keeps swinging. Back and forth. Back and forth.

We try to make sense of things that never will—the perpetual incongruence of what is fair and what is real. What is good and what is bad. These things never fit in tidy boxes, and still we try.

But here is the truth I keep finding: There is a space inside us that can reconcile the contrast. We have the strength to withstand the extremes.

We are the crucible. We take the good and the bad, what is fair and what is real, the incongruence of it all. And from it, we become something new. Something good, even.

It's been seventy days and here we are. Still living, still breathing, still hoping, still crying, still laughing, still screaming. We are shattered and melting. Growing and breaking.

We have the space for it all.

Everything, all at once.

||||||||||||||||||||||||

SEPTEMBER 25, 2020

There is beauty in it.

These days have been despair mixed with a terrible joy—the kind that aches and gnaws. It is a tragic elegance that makes you cry and feel so desperately alive at the same time.

"Beauty? What kind of heartless person says such a thing when their husband is fighting for his life in the ICU?"

No, this isn't a ransom I would elect to pay for foresight or wisdom. If I had a choice, I wouldn't pick this devastation.

And maybe it's just a truism I chant for self-preservation.

"There is beauty in it."

A clichéd life raft or a deep, philosophical truth?

I do not know.

But here we are, so here I am. At every intersection we are faced with a choice. It is in this agency we reckon with ourselves.

Yesterday I watched you sit on the edge of your bed unassisted. Painfully thin and shaking, you smiled the kind of smile that both excavates and buries—an enigmatic calamity that either suffocates or brings us up as something new.

Your smile, your grimace, your radiance, your pallor, your weakness, your strength. It was joy and it was pain wrapped up in that awful beauty and presented to me as a choice.

What did I see?

Platitudes of light and darkness, joy and sorrow are peeled down and given new meaning. It is in this pulpy mess we are made. It is here we decide whether we'll be smothered or take root.

Today you reached for my face with a hand too weak to make it. It was terrible and it was wonderful. That dizzying swing of everything all at once.

And somewhere in there, I had a choice.

Every day, I have a choice.

There is beauty in it.

IIIIIIIIIIIIIIIIIIIIIIII

OCTOBER 4, 2020

You scratched my head today.

You called at 7 a.m. saying you'd had a rough night. You said you felt weak and frail.

I got out of bed and came to see you.

You are pale and thin but still so beautiful. Still everything I could ever want.

You are too tired to brush your teeth. You apologize for your weakness and it brings me to my knees.

"Do you remember when squeezing my hand was enough to make me weep?" I ask.

But no, you don't. Today is all there is for you. There is no yesterday.

I turn on *The Office* and pull my chair next to your bed. I rest my forehead on your knee that is all bone.

And then, there it is. Your hand on the back of my head, gently scratching. Your fingers tremble but persist.

Scratch, scratch, scratch, then rest.

Scratch, scratch, scratch, then rest.

You are comforting me.

This, here, is all I ever wanted. Not a display of strength but a notion of presence. Maybe they are the same thing.

There you are.

Here we are, together.

There is nothing more on either side of this space.

Not then, but now. It all happens here.

Your weak hand on my head, tears streaming as I face away

from you, my teeth clenching the insides of my cheeks as I try to keep it together.

"Stay strong for him, Steph. Stay strong."

It's harder than you think. It's harder than I thought. I have sores on the insides of my mouth to prove it.

There is no poetry, just a stark precipice of feeling that is sometimes best left as it is. Exposed in its nakedness. Raw beauty that is the present.

The water, the well, the river, the bank, the pendulum—none of it matters here.

It's just you, me, your hand, my head.

Everything that ever happens is right now.

IIIIIIIIIIIIIIIIIIIIIII

OCTOBER 20, 2020

I am standing in an empty field. It is cold and barren. I look for warmth from the setting sun, but it is out of reach. I know it will be dark soon. A lonely chill is coming—a constant companion of nothingness that hums its lowly song, distant but ever present.

This is my grief. There is nothing unique about it. It is a universal malady that can't be understood until it is felt. And once it's felt, it binds us together. It is a hollow commiseration that burrows deep, a knowing that is never undone.

You sent me flowers for my birthday yesterday. From your hospital bed during your fifth round of chemotherapy, you sent me flowers.

The beauty and pain I saw in that bouquet was another empty field. It was loneliness and heartbreak, with happiness and beauty on the distant horizon. It was an echoing holler of unanswerable questions.

"Why us?" and "how much longer?" and "when do I break?"

You are getting better but it doesn't get any easier. Like anger, fear has a way of pushing us forward. It stalks and hunts. It keeps us moving. We are escaping a dark forest. Running, running, running from the monsters.

Once we make it to the field, exposed to the sadness of it all, there is nowhere left to hide. No tree to cower behind, no monsters to run from but the ones we carry with us. Just the expansive emptiness of sadness. It is the epicenter of alone.

But I am tired of moving and grief is a cunning beast. She is a different kind of monster—one that sits inside. There is no chase once we see it.

So I sit down in the grass. I know it is better to feel than to keep running. I lay my body down, surrounded by love but still lonely. I know it will be dark soon but I allow myself to rest anyways.

I cry.

I crack.

I break just enough so that the sun can make its way back in someday.

〜〜〜〜〜〜〜〜〜〜〜〜

OCTOBER 27, 2020

We are standing in an empty field.

In this universe, light is one of the few laws that evades relativity. Whether we run towards it or away from it, the speed with which light travels remains the same.

And I think: "How wonderful it would be to live like that, unequivocally consistent. Universally stable. Empirically unchanged by the things that run away from us."

But humans are not this way. We are built to shift, to mold, to crack, to permeate the subjective realities that are as ephemeral as they are tragic. This is the fabric of survival. Worlds and nations and cultures could not have evolved if we didn't bend.

So what of light? There has to be some lesson learned from its nature. Humans are constantly changing, but there is universality in us, too. I can feel it, though I can't quite put my finger on it.

And then it hits me, as I sit in this empty field. My journey is intrinsically lonely, but there is an absolute that makes it less so.

It is love.

Our love is the light. Consistent. Stable despite what comes towards us. Unchanged through the turbulence.

Here it is. A burning entity of knowing. An undeniable reality, constant and true. It seeps through our cracks. It binds us. There is nothing relative about it.

Humans bend but love persists.

The pendulum swings. The paradigm shifts.

And I think: "What a gift it is to walk through hell together."

Your hand on mine, my ribs resting against the cold plastic rail of your hospital bed as I lean as close to you as possible. I am not alone in this field. There's a dark forest between us but our love burns through it. Love is the bridge here.

I see it now.

Light is the conduit and love is the bridge.

||||||||||||||||||||||||

NOVEMBER 3, 2020

You were scared last night.

It is a unique form of tragedy to witness fear in someone of your stature. It's both a building and a breaking. It is catharsis and devastation.

I remember when my dad was scared, towards the end of his life. He wasn't afraid of dying. He was afraid we would forget him. I walked into his room one evening to find him sitting in his at-home hospital bed clutching a black-and-white photo of his mother.

I put an arm around his neck and he bent in towards me, sobbing. It is a strange feeling—to be a child comforting a parent. It is a revolving door of heartbreak and strength that takes years to push through.

But I remember thinking, all those years ago, "it takes a strong man to cry into his daughter's arms."

It takes bravery to confront the stark truths of emotion, to not stave them off in ironclad boxes, buried by ego and cushioned by denial.

How romantic it is to believe that courage is the absence of fear.

How truthful it is to say: I am strong and I am scared. These two truths need one another to exist, like light and darkness.

It isn't one or the other.

It is in the intersection of these empty fields that we confront ourselves: sad and strong and brave and weak and courageous and afraid. We are everything in these moments.

You cried on your hospital bed last night and it was that same undoing and rebuilding. I gave you a soft embrace, careful not to break you.

You, the immovable man that bends.

The kiln, the confluence, the cracks, the crucible—you are everything in this moment.

How strong you must be to show weakness.

How resilient you are to be afraid and persist.

ıııııııııııııııııı

NOVEMBER 12, 2020

Our girls.

I haven't dared write about them yet. My mind hasn't been ready to assess the guilt of that grief.

Oh, the weight of it. I try to cradle their emotions in my arms like shards of broken glass. They are impossible to hold but I try anyway. They shatter into fragments so small it's hard to tell whose is whose.

Is that your pain or mine? I don't know so I try to take it all.

I gather it up and put what is left of me back into the pieces that seep through my fingers like sand. I try to make them into something beautiful but there is no gold left inside me, no potter's hand to fuse them into something stronger.

There is a strength in knowing I am capable of holding my own sadness and a peculiar pain in knowing that I can't hold everyone else's.

I know the hollowness of childhood grief too well to ignore it. It burrows. It gnaws. It seeps and rots and burns, burns, burns.

I want to shield my girls from it. I want them to never know the sound of a guttural cry—one that comes from a depth so deep it echoes for eternity. I want to throw my body between them and the flames, to cast myself into the pit to stop the ringing.

I would do it. I would.

But I know I can't.

The flames flicker and the cries resound.

I fight against a knowing that I am intimately acquainted with: I cannot carry their grief. It is a solitary act. They need to do it alone.

They seem too young to walk those empty fields, but I know they have to.

Alone but not lonely.

Cloaked in love but crossing them in ways only they know how.

Cradled by their grandmothers' loving hands, encouraged by their grandfathers' wisdom both in heaven and on earth, surrounded by devoted aunts and uncles and cousins, bolstered by strangers who care so fiercely they've become family.

We've shattered into a million pieces, but love will make us gold again. I see what will sweep them back into some semblance of wholeness.

And it's not me.

There is carnal resistance to a mother admitting she doesn't have everything her child needs, but here it is: my grief is mine to carry alone, but theirs isn't.

It's not mine to carry alone.

It's not mine to carry.

|||||||||||||||||||||||||||

NOVEMBER 28, 2020

My girls.

I hope you will forgive me.

I hope you see how I'm trying to gather our pieces, scrambling to keep some semblance of us.

It's panning for gold. So much is sifting through the cracks.

I wish I could be around more.

Do you see my absence as love or abandonment?

Do you see me treading below the surface, pointing my toes to touch the bottom, to both breach for air and feel for solid ground?

I don't know if this looks like swimming or drowning to you.

Where are you, gravity?

Sometimes when I close my eyes there is an image in my mind. It is a silhouette of a woman walking uphill with a giant orb on the small of her back. She stoops under the weight of it.

Like Sisyphus she is pushing up, up, up only to have the weight roll back onto her.

It is crushing.

Oh, I feel you now, gravity.

You, that polar pull—sometimes friend and sometimes foe.

So is this swimming or is this drowning?

It's hard to know if I want to be grounded or weightless, to push forward or rest in that listless calm.

My girls.

I hope you will forgive me.

My searching seems to come up short. It's all just seeping through.

My strength isn't enough to carry the weight of it. It's all too heavy.

I only have the brawn to carry my own sadness.

I only have the power to come up for air.

All around me are hands outstretched, to pull me out or catch the weight of it. It is an orchestra of willing hands that I play into willingly.

I wish I was strong enough to do it alone but I'm not.

When you look back on these days, I hope you'll see that I was searching for gold and pushing forward and swimming not sinking.

And for all of this I hope you will forgive me.

My girls.

ıııııııııııııııııııııı

DECEMBER 12, 2020

Why?

The thief that lurks down every tragic alleyway.

I've not allowed myself to give in to her allure this time around. I know she is a dark road that forks and twists but never yields. She takes and takes. She is a highway of empty promises and unrequited love—the Silk Road of human experience. Gods were built on her back and she knows her power.

We navigate her course, hoping good works or altruism or even grace will give us clout.

But she is a one-way street.

And still we look over our shoulders. We retrace our steps,

desperately searching for where we went wrong or what we did right. And we are drawn to ask: why?

What did I do to deserve this?

For me, the answer came like an effigy in the night, distant but familiar: "Nothing, sweetheart. Nothing at all. And this is where the beauty lies, but it's up to you to find it."

There is no sacred text here. No divinity in suffering, no notion of reward for those strong enough to endure.

What a beautiful gift this is. What liberation is found when we recognize the bittersweet truth borne from the womb of grief.

Life is not a stark throughway of punishment and reward but a ruthless and forgiving stream of experience.

How tragically beautiful it is. You'd almost think it cruel if you couldn't see the sweetness in it all.

Sometimes there is no why. There is only what we choose to make of it. All of the power, all of the why is within us.

We are animals of agency but not everything in life is a consequence.

The other day you asked why. I wanted to give you some grandiose exposé on suffering and meaning. I wanted to tell you there was some sanctity in the pain.

But I know.

It just is what it is.

Once we can accept this, we can let go.

||||||||||||||||||||||||

DECEMBER 14, 2020

I'd do it all again if I knew.

I lay beside you last night, as I have every night since you came home. I listened to your breaths, short but steady as air filled your lungs without machines or medicine.

What a gift. What a gift.

I thought about all those days I sat beside you as you slept, my hand clutching yours, not knowing if you'd ever hold me back. I remember the beeps and wires and tubes and alarms and foggy eyes and half-cocked smiles calling for me from another world.

You reached for me. I know you did. I pulled you in and whispered their names and you followed me home.

And now you are here beside me, different but still as you always were.

What a gift. What a gift.

For all of the trauma and pain and uncertainty, of one thing I'm sure: I'd choose this over and over, every time.

I do not wear this admission like a martyr's badge. There is nothing unique about me.

You would do the same. You would.

Those who have felt this love know that grief is a small ransom to pay.

And here is the beauty of life—there is symmetry in all things.

The grand arbitrator of human existence: not fairness, but symmetry.

Balance, not justice.

The pendulum swings.

I find freedom as I arc with her: life, death, grief, love, joy, pain, sickness, health, suffocation, breath, broken, rebuilt.

It isn't fair but it is balanced.

She isn't just but there is beauty in her extremes and what we find in the spaces between.

It's all there if we choose to see it.

What a gift.

I'd choose you over and over to feel it all.

What a gift.

〰〰〰〰〰〰〰〰〰〰

DECEMBER 28, 2020

Your body.

The savage body that carried you through miles of uncharted trails—through the abyss of odds and dire statistics and nights of holding on.

"Just get him through till dawn."

What a statement.

What a burden.

What a gift.

Poked and stitched and mechanical when I was your voice and you were unaware. Twilight called asking for my permission to cut you open one more time. Just one more time.

And it was always "yes."

Yes.

A strange guilt built with each utterance of "do everything you can." There was a peculiar sense of selfishness that came when a new tube was put in, a new medication was administered, a new machine attached.

All because I couldn't fathom life with you not in it.

All because life is mundane until we see how special it is.

Looking at your body was a pulling of awe and culpability, joy and guilt. I am still sorting through the thick of it.

How much can one body take?

How much should one body take?

That question haunted and burrowed and festered for over one hundred days. It still takes hold.

I made the call for more when doctors first told me to let your body be. I screamed and pleaded and said: "More machines! More medicine! More tubes!"

I know it's what you wanted, but still.

There is trauma there.

But now here you are, alive and rebuilding. And I can't help but think about what a peculiar time it is to be living a battle so many are fighting right now.

Ventilators, ICUs, ECMO, beeps, pokes, infections, machines, sedation, advocates, life, death, and the guilt in between.

I am struck by our audacity to believe that living is a given. I am sobered by my prior confidence in the monotony of life.

Perhaps grief precipitates cliché, but here it is: life is precious.

And still, we write it off in the hundreds of thousands like some offshore account, hiding from the fact that dying is easier than living.

The only guilt in this life is taking it for granted.

Your body is a miracle.

Cherish the gift. Every moment. Every breath.

ıııııııııııııııııııııı

JANUARY 3, 2021

2020.

I've taken my time. I've reflected and reached and begged to understand.

I am expecting to feel anger for you and all I find is nostalgia.

A melancholy, quiet and sweet.

There is no screaming, just a simple acceptance of life for doing what she does: giving and taking and benevolently teaching love through pain to a world that has become comfortably numb.

How do you long for a year that has brought such sorrow?

How do you miss a time you'd never choose to relive?

In Portuguese there is a word for this dichotomy. It has no English translation because it is better felt than explained.

Saudade.

A melancholic longing for difficult times.

Sad times.

Simpler times.

A time when everything was stripped bare, teaching us that meaning lies in the very things we take for granted.

Sadness humbles. It cracks us open, allowing us to see others' pain in ways that happiness can't. It teaches us about the universality of suffering, but more importantly, the transcendent power of love.

A love that is often overlooked without the presence of grief.

Life, the pendulum.

The arc of duality that both gently and forcefully reminds us of the importance of balance. If we don't listen, she bellows.

Perhaps one day we'll all look back on this year with saudade.

Maybe we'll see it as a time of growth for a world that stopped listening to these simple truths.

We are all connected.

You are stronger than you think.

And love.

Love.

Love.

Love.

||||||||||||||||||||||||||

JANUARY 4, 2021

I am a tree.

I knew it when I put my hand on your lungs and felt an aching in my legs.

It flowed through me and down to the ground.

I rooted myself for stability.

I laid my feet flat on the hospital floor and grounded myself to the earth, growing into the network that was there waiting to absorb the suffering.

Energy cannot be destroyed, after all.

It has to go somewhere.

And like a season your pain was converted.

It churned and it burned.

It rotted and decomposed and it turned into love.

It turned into power.

Like a revenant it came back to me in blooms of perennial knowing: pain is love and love is pain.

It is all a delicate cycle.

How terrible and beautiful it is to be a tree.

‖‖‖‖‖‖‖‖‖‖‖‖‖‖‖‖‖‖‖

JANUARY 9, 2021

Your body.

I watched it transform in front of my eyes, from beard and glow and glistening muscle to skin and bones.

Right there on that hospital bed you metamorphosed.

It was earthly to eternal.

It was finite to ethereal.

It was soldier to warrior.

And I say this in all sincerity, despite what I know you see in the mirror: you are stronger now.

I wish there were sentences powerful enough to describe the tenacity of your spirit. I wish I could splay them out and package them up in an offering that would do justice to that soul of yours, the one I watched claw its way through the cosmos and back into this world.

The one I watched growl and revolt and rage, rage, rage, rage against the dying of the light.

There is no greater feat, no more colloidal showing of bravery than to stare death in the face and say the words "not today."

Because I was there when you made your presence known to the other side.

I felt it.

I knew it.

I did.

You chose life and I sat by your side, day after day as you ran through realms of order and chaos, life and decay.

All while you slept.

Your body withered, but your soul . . . Your soul.

Your soul was both impermeable and porous.

It was here and there.

It was a vessel for an interminable spark that caught fire while you slept, awakening all manner of beasts inside us.

And I ran alongside you, screaming our battle cry with hearts ablaze.

Not today.

Not today.

Not today.

It was your soul, not your body, that did that.

You are stronger now.

|||||||||||||||||||||||

JANUARY 12, 2021

And if I am a tree then you are the branches
growing up towards the light
in cycles and seasons
hosting leaves that wither and bloom.

There is sanctuary here,
together in the darkness and decay
and silence.

It is in this intercession,
in the blinkered prelude before regrowth,
that we learn:
we all started as seeds on the forest floor.

There is a time to be the root
and a time to be the branch.

And so for now I will tether you.

‖‖‖‖‖‖‖‖‖‖‖‖‖‖‖‖‖‖‖

JANUARY 18, 2021

I am a ship out at sea, unmoored but afloat, somehow.

I navigate the squall of grief, bow bending under the weight of memory.

So this is what it means to relive trauma, to recall the things we wish would sink.

These are the things that need to resurface in order to heal. They are an anchor but come up as gold, piece by piece, if we let them.

I now see that this can only be done with land in sight.

So I dive.

It comes and goes in waves—those reminiscent feelings of hourly uncertainty, of dipping pressures and racing heartbeats and lowered oxygen.

I remember.

They rose and fell like a winter swell, drowning you in your sleep.

And all I could do was watch from your bedside, clinging to the mast as you blew through the storm.

I remember.

The scorching in my chest with each alarm, like coming up for air a little too late.

That sound will haunt me forever.

I'm sorry I wasn't strong enough to stay in the room.

I'm sorry I let fear drag me down.

She was an eddy of staggering power and I wasn't strong enough to swim out.

I'd leave your side with the resounding feeling of failure. I hadn't been able to stem the tide.

But strength is an ocean. It ebbs and crests and crashes and calms. It is both powerful and soft.

It can be everything all at once.

And as I dive it whispers to me on the wings of a forgiving current: "Be soft with yourself. You would have sunk if you had tried to steer through the thick of it all at once."

And I remember.

Some days we are trees, rooted and strong enough to weather the storm.

Other days we are shipwrecked on a vengeful ocean, just trying to stay afloat.

That is grief.

This is healing.

I remember.

||||||||||||||||||||||||

JANUARY 22, 2021

"Don't let it harden you."

You speak to me. It is a gentle voice I cannot place. At times it's like a dream that comes back to me in pieces. You are a distant ship on the horizon and I strain to pull you in.

Other times it wells inside me—a booming expression of knowing.

How can something be so foreign and so familiar? You sound like a '70s song my father used to sing—a secondhand melody that has become my own.

Whoever you are, I listen. I will not pretend to know your source but I do know you are real.

You were my saving grace, a solvent of fear on the hardest days. Behind the cacophony of uncertainty and that horrible mask of catatony you were always there. You were an undertone of hope in the darkest times. You declared yourself in liminal fire, in those spaces between that are only found in the tremors of grief.

You stood in the flames and made yourself heard as everything burned down around me.

You said: "He is going to live."

"There is beauty in it."

"Be soft with yourself."

And, "Love, love, love, love."

What another cruel irony, that understanding is discovered in the depths of despair.

That true love is appreciated in the face of loss.

You held me in tragedy like a coat of arms, guarding against the words "end of life." You told me he would stay and I listened. I melted into you and you carried me.

I was never alone.

You were the pendulum, the river, the water, the well, the flame, the sea, the kiln, the roots, and the branches.

You were everything all at once.

And now you speak to me again, though your voice is fading as the pain recedes.

Even now I know it is impossible to live with a heart cracked open. We barter comfort for knowing and I shamelessly submit to the solace.

But I still hear you, for now, distant though you may be. I will hold on to you as long as I can. I'll cling to the rope as you drift away.

You say: "Don't let it harden you. Tragedy is a thief but only if we allow it. Make sure to fill the cracks with gold not embers. Let pain make you stronger, not corrosive."

I hear you.

I know you, hero of my childhood and ghost of my adolescence.

It was always you.

|||||||||||||||||||||||||

JANUARY 30, 2021

Or has it always been me?

Someone once told me that all the power I'd ever need was already inside me. That gods and kingdoms, light and love, forgiveness and redemption were all gateways—analogues in the search for ourselves. They were kindling that needed only a spark of self-belief to ignite into the ferocious flame that has always lived in the bowels of our souls.

And still we send ships out into the night, searching for sources of light when it's been inside us all along.

It's a crusade to believe in yourself. It's a voyage of tumultuous enmity to seek out the strength that lives inside. We grow out, not up, questioning ourselves and tethering to extraneous forces for stability.

But I was a tree before I knew it. My roots were already taking hold even before I blew on the embers of my soul—before the smoke signals of my power billowed up and out, allowing me to see what was already inside: power, strength, stamina, patience, and oh—that love, love, love, love.

Some have asked how I do it—how I navigate the waters of grief and motherhood with seeming resolve. Ironically, I remember asking my mother the same question after she cared for my younger brother when he had leukemia, and after she held my own father's hand when cancer took him all those years ago, when I was a child.

Her response always seemed trite, but now mine is the same: "You just do it."

Maybe she felt a knowing she couldn't describe—that there is an infinite well inside us. It is a pipeline of strength accessed only by the deepest of sorrows. It is unique to our suffering and yet its source is the same. We can call it heaven or spirit, nirvana or oxytocin, god, or chemistry. We've fought wars over her definition, but it's all just this: love.

An everlasting spring of stability that feeds us. Through the most uncertain times, it connects us in a relentless stream of calm.

All the power we ever need is inside us because we are connected to that infinite fount.

Love. Is. Power.

I was never alone.

It's always been you.

But you were right—it's always been me, too.

It's always been everything all at once.

||||||||||||||||||||||

FEBRUARY 26, 2021

I had a dream about you all those months ago, when you were in the in-between.

It was a simple dream.

We were lying on a bed that was not our own. It was midmorning and the sun was glowing through white curtains that billowed in a forgiving breeze. Your beard was coming through in patches. Your eyes were tired but resolute, having just traveled a thousand lives from a hospital bed.

We were laughing softly about some inside joke and the girls were playing in a tree out back.

I looked at you intently, acknowledging the miracle of asking "do you want more coffee?" and you answering "no, let's stay here a while." What could be better than this?

I laid my head on your chest, gently, so as not to put pressure on your weakened frame. My head rose with each inhale and I remember marveling at your lungs as they breathed, working and living on their own.

I woke up with tears streaming down my face. At the time you were in the midst of the storm—sedated, struggling, drowning.

You were a cold and swollen hand I clung to, like my grip alone could keep you here. I would have given almost anything to live in that moment with you, awake and talking and breathing.

Living on your own.

But you were a dream a hundred choices away.

You were a hope that lived only in the frailty of my imagination.

But now here you are, awake and talking and breathing.

And here we are, lying on a bed that is not our own, relishing the ether of now.

Today.

This moment, it begs us.

Don't waste it.

Dreams are made of chests that rise and fall, of voices that laugh softly saying "What could be better than this?"

IIIIIIIIIIIIIIIIIIIIIIIII

FEBRUARY 24, 2021

Fifty-three scars.

Last week I watched Poppy practice her counting skills on your skin. Reading your wounds like braille, she followed them with an index finger too small to understand the vastness of their highs and lows, too new to pain to recognize the distance between them. A cartographer in the landscape of trauma, she stopped at "eleventeen," and you helped her along, all the way to fifty-three.

Your body is a topography of bravery, from the white nicks

on the side of your skull where the tubes were fused, to the deep rounded grooves in your heels carved by the pressure of motionless sedation.

And just like that you become a new man. You are an entire world sculpted by the expansion of grief and solidified by the bedrock of rebirth.

And just like that our little girls are forged into strong women. Though they don't know it yet, they are crusaders in the badlands of eroding hope. They are pioneers in the rediscovery of you, and through you, they learn to navigate the channels of sorrow caused by your fight.

They are just as savage as your scars, negotiating the plateau of unknowns and calderas of dreamless sleep with absolute fearlessness.

It will take years for them to realize the voyagers you have made of them. It will be a basin of persistent damming before they understand the geology of your scars.

But in the end, as with all things rock or human—across millennia or lifetimes lived in a single tragedy—the pressure will make them stronger.

Fifty-three scars that rise and fall, each one a distinct memory we will recall like familiar landscapes in a foreign land.

If ever there was a road map of courage, this would be it—your skin and their small fingers, tracing the great divide.

⁓⁓⁓⁓⁓⁓⁓⁓

FEBRUARY 28, 2021

Because I was a voyager, too.

I was a small hand on my own father's gray and sinking skin, all those years ago. I traced scars with fingers too young to count the vastness of sorrow. I was a settler on the fault lines of hope and heartbreak, my flag a tattered emblem of love that took years to reclaim its home.

I crossed oceans to get away from myself, from small hands that understood the outline of pain. I was an explorer campaigning for anything other than faith and sunken skin, searching for anywhere but here.

When I landed, I became a master of ramparts and walls. I was a fortress of persistent damming, staving off the flood that was sure to come with the slightest crack.

When the levee broke, it was a deluge of despair. For a time, I was hauled away in the humbling current of reckoning. There was no up or down, no here or there—just a suffocating ache that clawed and retched.

I was pulled and dragged but always held, somehow.

And it was here I learned that strength isn't found in walls and fortresses. Like water, love is a bastion of power that isn't brick and mortar. She is impenetrable because she lets everything in and everything out. In her, there is room for it all—an unending tide of now.

She is everything all at once.

My girls, here is the foundation of your strength. You will be pioneers in the rediscovery of yourselves, anchored by small hands that understand sorrow, held by the porous current of love.

You will be hauled and drowned and tossed in the memory of tragedy. As a mother I am steeling myself for the flood.

But I know that with those hands you will crawl on the shores of empathy with a depth and knowing that are only found in the rifts of grief.

You will plant your flag in foreign lands that speak of a familiar love. You will let everything in, and everything out. You will have room for it all—you are unending tides of now.

And although you'd never choose this pain, you will know that there was never any other way for you.

Your path was always tracing the great divide.

I know this, my girls.

Because I was a voyager too.

⸻

MARCH 31, 2021

I am stronger now.

I pay no homage to stoicism, only to sharp edges and cracked surfaces, to long cries behind closed closet doors and growling screams into mascara-stained pillows.

Feeling it all—maybe that is what it means to stay strong.

In fractured utterances it seeps out of me, and I am stronger now.

I am angry and devastated and overwhelmed. I am happy and grateful and overjoyed.

I feel it all—the geyser of hot emotion that becomes a cesspool if it doesn't break ground, if it never finds air.

This is the new pendulum.

When it arced on you, I didn't feel the weight of me.

And now here I am, a heavy swing of the past eight months, smoke signals on a yawning horizon.

I awake in twilight mired in fear. I allow myself to feel it. I know it is part of the process. Part of healing. Part of the power that comes from allowing myself to be fragile, part of acknowledging that human frailty is the great mason of becoming.

Through the brick and mortar of my reckoning I bow and bend.

I crack and break.

I am the sum of my fissures that bleed and breathe.

And I think: maybe strength isn't holding things together, but knowing when to fall apart.

EPILOGUE

In total, Rivs was in the ICU for one hundred and one days, beginning on July 2, 2020, with his admission to the Flagstaff Medical Center. He was life flighted to HonorHealth Scottsdale Shea Medical Center on July 24 and remained in their ICU until October 7, when he was transferred to the bone marrow transplant unit, down the hallway at the same facility.

Over his three and a half months in the ICU, he endured four rounds of chemotherapy—most of which happened while he was fully sedated and unaware of his cancer diagnosis. Once sedative medications were no longer administered, by August 3, it would take three weeks for him to "wake" from his induced coma. By August 25, he was responding to commands and communicating with eye movements and subtle hand squeezes. Still hooked to ECMO and a tracheal ventilator, he was unable to speak orally for several weeks. He was completely immobile, having lost total control of his neck and limbs due to muscle wasting. He learned to communicate via lip-reading and, later, by sign language and writing on a dry-erase board.

After working daily with speech pathology, Rivs was eventually able to speak on a Passy-Muir valve, a small one-way valve placed between the tracheostomy and ventilator tubes. His first words were "I want Sprite" followed by "the titration of my IV potassium is too concentrated." That is how I knew, without a doubt, that Rivs was still in there. During this time, despite his coherence, his chance of survival remained poor due to the massive tumor burden in his lungs.

At the end of August, Rivs started daily sessions with physical and occupational therapists, working to regain movement of his fingers, hands, feet, and legs. On September 10, sixty-eight days after his initial hospitalization, Rivs sat on his bedside with the assistance of eight medical workers, still hooked to ECMO and the ventilator. Two days later, he stood upright for fifteen seconds while fully supported and strapped to a rotating hospital bed. He was the second patient in the hospital's history to stand vertically while on ECMO.

Over the subsequent seven weeks, Rivs suffered from severe ICU delirium. On many days, delirium compromised his ability to recognize me or to understand why he had been hospitalized. Most mornings I'd come in to find him awake, confused, and restrained to his bed. He'd beg me to take him home, to break him free, to bring him his bike so he could ride home, and I would have to explain that he was still very sick and unable to stand on his own. For me, it was the most traumatic part of his illness.

On September 21, 2020, sixty-eight days from when he was first placed on the machine, Rivs was removed from the ECMO circuit. Eight days later, after having been on life support for eighty-nine days, he was decannulated from the ventilator. Four rounds of SMILE chemotherapy (still with the omission of L-asparaginase and a 50 percent dose of methotrexate) had killed enough lung tumors for him to breathe on his own, with supplemental high-dose oxygen.

On October 5, Rivs stood on his own two legs, with the assistance of a Sara Stedy lift while still in the ICU.

He was transferred to the bone marrow transplant unit on October 7, where he would spend three weeks receiving another round of chemotherapy at full dose, with the addition of pegaspargase (a less toxic substitute for L-asparaginase). By the time he made it to the bone marrow transplant unit, Rivs had lost over seventy pounds—almost

40 percent of his bodyweight—ultimately weighing in at ninety-five pounds at a height of six feet one.

Due to his tracheostomy, through which he still received high-flow oxygen, he was unable to eat or drink by mouth. In total, he was unable to eat solid food for a total of one hundred thirty days.

After completing his fourth round of chemo in the bone marrow transplant unit, on November 14, 2020, Rivs was transferred from HonorHealth to a physical rehabilitation hospital, where he spent two weeks learning how to walk, use the bathroom, and feed himself. On November 21, he took his first steps, from his hospital bed to the bathroom, assisted by a walker and two physical therapists.

He was discharged from the rehab hospital and came home to my care on November 28, four and a half months after his initial hospitalization. At that time, he was mainly fed through a PEG feeding tube in his stomach and could hardly walk from the bed to the bathroom. He required constant oxygen support and could only move forward a few steps with the assistance of a walker.

Rivs underwent a final round of chemotherapy in December 2020. Soon after, he was deemed unfit to receive a bone marrow transplant or any additional chemotherapy. After careful consideration, Dr. Briggs and Dr. Fauble decided that, due to Rivs's lack of mobility, compromised lung function, and severe malnutrition, his odds of dying from the transplant were higher than his risk of cancer relapse. At the time, his risk of relapse was 90 percent.

In January 2021, weakened by the months of immobility and the caustic effects of chemotherapy, Rivs was unable to take more than five steps at a time. Furthermore, a pulmonary function test performed at the end of December found his lung function to be at 20 percent capacity. Dr. Fauble and Briggs concluded that continuing to cycle through chemo would not be beneficial, as it would only continue to cause weight loss and further compromise his lungs.

On January 6, 2021, Rivs ended his cancer treatment.

A PET scan performed mid-January found no evidence of disease. Though his lungs were permanently scarred from the massive tumor burden and high levels of oxygen over an extended period of time, Rivs was in remission.

In November of the same year, Rivs walked the entire twenty-six point two miles of the New York City Marathon.

It took him nine hours and thirty-six minutes.

In April 2022, he completed the Boston Marathon in six hours and thirty-one minutes.

To this day, Rivs's care team considers his case a medical miracle. His survival would have been impossible without the tireless work of his team of doctors, nurses, respiratory therapists, physical therapists, occupational therapists, speech pathologists, dieticians, flight nurses, and hospital transfer coordinators.

They walked the tightrope between art and science. They believed.

And it was beautiful.

It was a miracle.